W9-CEL-770

How to Use This Book

Look for these special features in this book:

SIDEBARS, **CHARTS**, **GRAPHS**, and original **MAPS** expand your understanding of what's being discussed—and also make useful sources for classroom reports.

FAQs answer common **F**requently **A**sked **Q**uestions about people, places, and things.

WOW FACTORS offer "Who knew?" facts to keep you thinking.

TRAVEL GUIDE gives you tips on exploring the state—either in person or right from your chair!

PROJECT ROOM provides fun ideas for school assignments and incredible research projects. Plus, there's a guide to primary sources—what they are and how to cite them.

Please note: All statistics are as up-to-date as possible at the time of publication.

Consultants: P. C. Anderson, Professor of History, Clemson University; Scott Brame, Professor of Geology, Clemson University; William Loren Katz

Book production by The Design Lab

Library of Congress Cataloging-in-Publication Data
Somervill, Barbara A.
 South Carolina / by Barbara A. Somervill.
    p. cm.—(America the beautiful. Third series)
 Includes bibliographical references and index.
 ISBN-13: 978-0-531-18591-9
 ISBN-10: 0-531-18591-5
 1. South Carolina—Juvenile literature. I. Title. II. Series.
 F269.3.S66 2009
 975.7—dc22   2007031030

No part of this publication may be reproduced in whole or in part, or stored in a retrieval system, or transmitted in any form or by any means, electronic, mechanical, photocopying, recording, or otherwise, without written permission of the publisher. For information regarding permission, write to Scholastic Inc., 557 Broadway, New York, NY 10012.

©2009 Scholastic Inc.
All rights reserved. Published in 2009 by Children's Press, an imprint of Scholastic Inc.
Published simultaneously in Canada. Printed in the United States of America.
SCHOLASTIC, CHILDREN'S PRESS, and associated logos are trademarks and/or registered trademarks of Scholastic Inc.

1 2 3 4 5 6 7 8 9 10 R 18 17 16 15 14 13 12 11 10 09

AMERICA ★ THE ★ BEAUTIFUL

South Carolina

BY BARBARA A. SOMERVILL

Third Series

Children's Press®
An Imprint of Scholastic Inc.
New York ★ Toronto ★ London ★ Auckland ★ Sydney
Mexico City ★ New Delhi ★ Hong Kong
Danbury, Connecticut

CONTENTS

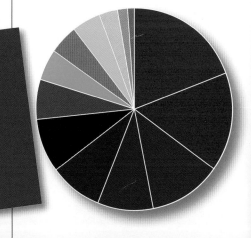

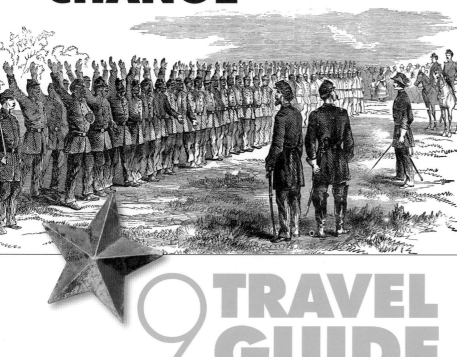

TENNESSEE

NORTH CAROLINA

Chattooga River

Shoeless Joe Jackson
Memorial Park

Chattooga

ROCK HILL

SPARTANBURG

GREENVILLE

Piedmont Plateau

Cherokee Path

Mann-Simons
Cottage

Sand Hills
State Forest

National Stock Car
Hall of Fame

Watered

Lynches

Pee Dee

SOUTH CAROLINA

★ **COLUMBIA**

Columbia State
Capitol

Congaree Swamp
National Monument

Lake
Marion

Black

Santee

Alligator
Adventure

MYRTLE
BEACH

Brookgreen
Gardens

Lake
Moultrie

Battery Park

CHARLESTON

Intracoastal
Waterway

Savannah

Edisto

Fort Sumter

GEORGIA

Parris Island
Museum

Sea Islands

HILTON HEAD BEACH

ATLANTIC
OCEAN

QUICK FACTS

State capital: Columbia
Largest city: Columbia
Total area: 32,020 square miles
(82,931 sq km)
Highest point: Sassafras Mountain,
3,560 feet (1,085 m) located in
Pickens County
Lowest point: Sea level along the
Atlantic Ocean

0   40
Miles

Welcome to South Carolina!

HOW DID SOUTH CAROLINA GET ITS NAME?

In 1629, King Charles I of England granted a large region in what is now the southeastern United States to Sir Robert Heath. The grant called the region Carolana after the Latin version of Charles (*Carolanus*). King Charles II changed the name to Carolina in 1663. In 1729, Carolina was split into two sections: North and South Carolina. The southern region has been called South Carolina ever since.

SOUTH
CAROLINA

ATLANTIC
OCEAN

8

READ ABOUT

Sunrise at
Litchfield Beach

LAND LAND LAND LAND

CHAPTER ONE

LAND

★

FROM ITS LOW-LYING SWAMPS TO ITS FORESTED FOOTHILLS, SOUTH CAROLINA OFFERS A VARIETY OF LANDSCAPES. Covering 32,020 square miles (82,931 square kilometers), the state is triangular in shape, bordered by only two states and an ocean. Not far from the northwestern corner of the state, South Carolina's highest point, Sassafras Mountain, rises 3,560 feet (1,085 meters) in Pickens County. The lowest point is sea level along the coast, where the rolling waves of the Atlantic Ocean crash onto beautiful beaches.

State Geo-Facts

Along with the state's geographical highlights, this chart ranks South Carolina's land, water, and total area compared to all other states.

Total area; rank . . . . 32,020 square miles (82,931 sq km); 40th
Land; rank . . . . 30,110 square miles (77,985 sq km); 40th
Water; rank . . . . 1,911 square miles (4,949 sq km); 21st
Inland water; rank . . . . 1,008 square miles (2,611 sq km); 21st
Coastal water; rank . . . . 72 square miles (186 sq km); 18th
Territorial water; rank . . . . 831 square miles (2,152 sq km); 11th
Geographic center . . . Richland, 13 miles (21 km) southeast of Columbia
Latitude . . . . 32°5' N to 35°25' N
Longitude . . . . 78°50' W to 83°40' W
Highest point . . . . .Sassafras Mountain, 3,560 feet (1,085 m)
. . . . .located in Pickens County
Lowest point . . . . Sea level along the Atlantic Ocean
Largest city . . . . .Columbia
Longest river . . . . .Savannah River, 238 miles (383 km)

Source: U.S. Census Bureau

 **South Carolina would fit inside Alaska, the largest state, 21 times.**

LAND REGIONS

South Carolina is divided into three distinct land regions. The largest is the Coastal Plain, which covers two-thirds of the state. The Piedmont includes most of the other one-third, with the Blue Ridge accounting for just 2 percent of South Carolina land.

The Coastal Plain

In South Carolina, the Coastal Plain extends more than 100 miles (161 km) inland. Most of the Coastal Plain is covered with either sand or clay. In general, the land is flat and close to sea level in elevation. The sands

South Carolina Topography

Use the color-coded elevation chart to see on the map South Carolina's high points (dark red to orange) and low points (green to dark green). Elevation is measured as the distance above or below sea level.

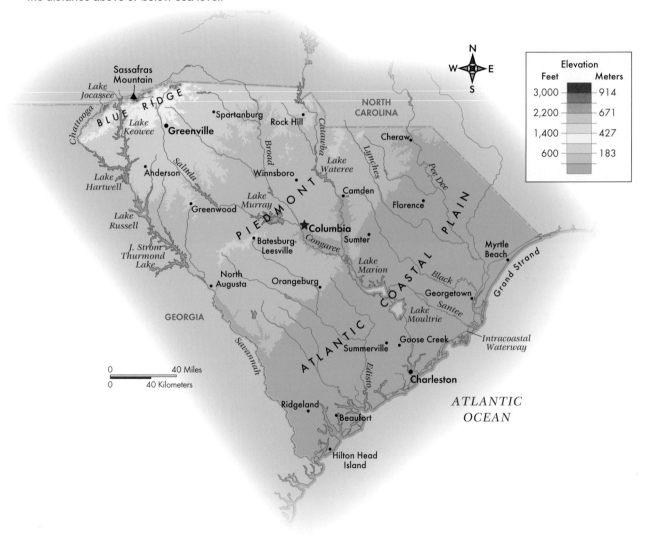

and clays that compose the Coastal Plain were deposited in alternating layers as ocean levels rose and fell over millions of years. Wherever you see Coastal Plain **sediments**, you are looking at an area that was covered by an ocean sometime in the last 65 million years.

WORD TO KNOW

sediments *material eroded from rocks and deposited elsewhere by wind, water, or glaciers*

A great egret wades in a saltwater marsh near Mount Pleasant.

The Coastal Plain has two main sections, the Inner and the Outer Coastal Plain. Along the Outer Coastal Plain, swamps and marshes once covered a large portion of the coast. Over the centuries, many of these natural wetlands were drained to make farmland. But some swamps and marshes remain, providing homes for herons, egrets, cottonmouth snakes, alligators, and many other creatures. The northern coast of South Carolina is a stretch of more than 60 miles (97 km) of uninterrupted beaches known as the Grand Strand.

The Outer Coastal Plain also includes more than 35 barrier islands, also called the Sea Islands. Scientists still debate how these islands formed. One theory says that they were once attached to the land and that thousands of years ago the sea rose and filled the valleys between the high points in the land. The high points became barrier islands, such as Kiawah, Isle of Palms, Hilton Head, and Sullivan's Island.

The Inner Coastal Plain features slow-moving rivers, pine forests, and relatively flat land. The rise from sea level is gradual, with most of this region lying between 200 and 400 feet (61 and 122 m) above sea level.

A region called the Sandhills lies along the border between the Coastal Plain and the Piedmont. The soil is dry and has few **nutrients**. Scientists believe these hills are the remnants of sand dunes that were deposited by the ocean between 5 million and 23 million years ago.

The Piedmont

The Piedmont is an upland **plateau** that covers the area between the fall line and the Blue Ridge Mountains. The region also contains monadnocks, single mountains rising above the surrounding land. Paris Mountain and Glassy Mountain are monadnocks in the upper Piedmont.

WORDS TO KNOW

nutrients *substances that nourish a plant or animal*

plateau *an elevated part of the earth with steep slopes*

A forest of oak trees on Spring Island

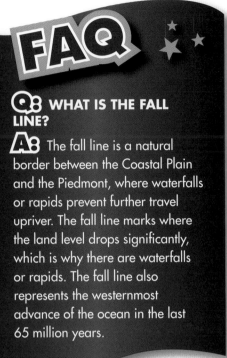

FAQ

Q8 WHAT IS THE FALL LINE?

A8 The fall line is a natural border between the Coastal Plain and the Piedmont, where waterfalls or rapids prevent further travel upriver. The fall line marks where the land level drops significantly, which is why there are waterfalls or rapids. The fall line also represents the westernmost advance of the ocean in the last 65 million years.

Table Rock Mountain is part of a state park that was developed by the Civilian Conservation Corps in the 1930s.

The Piedmont enjoys cooler temperatures and less humidity than the Coastal Plain. The soil is generally richer but is clay based as opposed to the sandy soils of the Coastal Plain. The landscape is gentle rolling hills, many of which are covered by hardwood forest.

The Blue Ridge

The Blue Ridge is the state's smallest region. The Blue Ridge Mountains are old, heavily covered with forest and cut by rivers. In many places, rivers plunge off cliffs in lacy waterfalls, such as Slicking Falls, Chau-Ram Falls, Licklog Falls, Pigpen Falls, and Dripping Rock. The autumn colors in the Blue Ridge are spectacular. Golden oak leaves flutter against the deep reds of maples and dark greens of pines. Table Rock State Park is one of seven state parks that lie in the Blue Ridge. The focal point of the park is Table Rock Mountain,

where the Cherokee people say the Great Spirit once sat down to dine, seated on the smaller peak nearby. Caesars Head, another Blue Ridge park, receives 79 inches (201 centimeters) of rain per year, the most of any place in the state.

LAKES, RIVERS, AND SWAMPS

Three large rivers flow from the uplands to the Atlantic. The Pee Dee River reaches the sea at Winyah Bay in northern South Carolina. Several shallow, slow-moving rivers—such as the Little Pee Dee, the Waccamaw, the Black, and the Lynches—flow into the Pee Dee. The Santee River runs 143 miles (230 km) across the state, from the Piedmont to the Atlantic Ocean. The Santee's **tributaries** include the Pacolet, Enoree, Tyger, Reedy, Saluda, and Wateree rivers.

A number of dams in the Santee River system have created some of the state's largest lakes, including Greenwood, Murray, Marion, and Moultrie. Lake Marion, the largest lake completely in the state, was created in 1942.

The Savannah River runs along the border between South Carolina and Georgia. The river has been dammed in several places in order to produce hydroelectric power. These dams also created a number of lakes, including Keowee and Jocassee.

Rivers that begin in the Coastal Plain are blackwater rivers. Their flow is slow. They carry little silt or sand and are fairly clear. The state's blackwater rivers include the Waccamaw, the Salkehatchie, the Combahee, and the Edisto.

South Carolina has more swampland than any other state except Louisiana. Several of the state's swamps are now parks or preserves. The Four Holes Swamp has the

WORD TO KNOW

tributaries *smaller rivers that flow into a larger river*

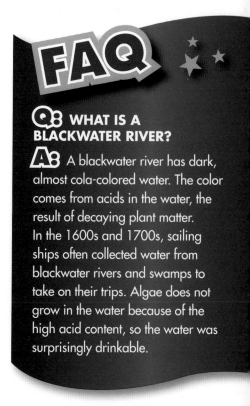

FAQ

Q8 WHAT IS A BLACKWATER RIVER?

A8 A blackwater river has dark, almost cola-colored water. The color comes from acids in the water, the result of decaying plant matter. In the 1600s and 1700s, sailing ships often collected water from blackwater rivers and swamps to take on their trips. Algae does not grow in the water because of the high acid content, so the water was surprisingly drinkable.

SEE IT HERE!

CONGAREE NATIONAL PARK

Congaree National Park contains 22,000 acres (8,900 hectares) of ancient cypress trees, including some of the tallest cypresses in the nation. The park provides habitat for 90 varieties of trees and 173 species of birds, as well as deer, raccoons, river otters, turtles, and snakes. Congaree has hiking trails and canoeing trails, along with a boardwalk that many visitors enjoy.

WORD TO KNOW

precipitation *all water that falls to the earth, including rain, sleet, hail, snow, dew, fog, or mist*

largest stand of old-growth bald cypress and tupelo gum trees in the world. Many are more than 1,000 years old. South Carolina's swamps are also home to swarms of buzzing mosquitoes and some skulking alligators.

CLIMATE

South Carolinians enjoy mild winters and swelter through hot, sticky summers. Most of the state receives between 46 and 50 inches (117 and 127 cm) of **precipitation** yearly, predominantly rain. Snow generally falls on the Blue Ridge and the Piedmont a few times each year. Summer brings dramatic rainstorms and occasional flash floods, particularly in the Piedmont.

Temperatures drop to freezing only in December, January, and February. South Carolinians can dine outside in November in most places in the state, and spring flowers often emerge as early as mid-February. But by summer, it is miserably hot. The Columbia area,

Weather Report

This chart shows record temperatures (high and low) for the state, as well as average temperatures (July and January) and average annual precipitation.

Record high temperature . . . . 111°F (44°C) in Blackville on September 4, 1925; at Calhoun Falls on September 8, 1925; and at Camden on June 28, 1954
Record low temperature . . . . –19°F (–28°C) at Caesars Head on January 21, 1985
Average July temperature . . . . 82°F (28°C)
Average January temperature . . . . 48°F (9°C)
Average yearly precipitation . . . . .51 inches (130 cm)

Source: National Climatic Data Center, NESDIS, NOAA, U.S. Dept. of Commerce

Evacuation route signs, like this one in Myrtle Beach, guide residents and visitors away from areas where hurricanes are expected to make landfall.

in the center of the state, is frequently the hottest place in South Carolina.

PLANT LIFE

In the 1500s, nearly all of what is now South Carolina was covered with forests. Today, forests cover about 65 percent of the state. Along the coast, a variety of pines, including loblolly pines and longleaf pines, dominate the forests. Bald cypress and tupelo gums grow in swamp areas. In the upstate, a mixed oak-hickory forest dominates, where oaks, hickories, gums, pines, maples, elms, and sycamores are common. Across the state, spring brings the delicate blossoms of dogwoods to

NATURAL DISASTERS

South Carolinians have endured some serious natural disasters. Tornadoes can strike at any time and sometimes come in clusters. On March 28, 1984, 22 tornadoes hit North and South Carolina, causing 57 deaths, hundreds of injuries, and serious property damage.

Hurricanes are a threat along the coast. To develop, they require warm ocean temperatures and strong winds. The winds swirl in a circular motion, gaining speed and power as the storm builds. Between 1900 and 2004, South Carolina suffered 15 direct hits from major hurricanes. In 1893, a devastating hurricane struck the Sea Islands. Between 1,000 and 2,000 people died in the hurricane, mostly from drowning. Another 30,000 were left without homes, and many thousands were injured.

Hurricane Hugo, which struck in 1989, was the costliest hurricane in South Carolina's history. It resulted in more than $7 billion in damage and left thousands of people without power, fresh water, or safe housing. Dozens of residents were killed. Many others were likely saved by an early hurricane warning system that advised them to leave the area before the storm hit.

ENDANGERED SPECIES

South Carolina has 22 animals and 19 plants that are listed as either **threatened** or **endangered**. Animals range from the eastern puma to the Florida manatee. Wood storks, bald eagles, and piping plovers are on the state's list, along with the Indiana bat. Five sea turtle species swim in South Carolina's waters. Injured leatherbacks, loggerheads, and hawksbills, along with green turtles and Kemp's ridley turtles, are cared for at the Sea Turtle Rehabilitation Center attached to the South Carolina Aquarium. Endangered and threatened plants include the small whorled pogonia, the rough-leaved loosestrife, and Schweinitz's sunflower. Also on the endangered list is the mountain sweet pitcher plant—a maroon, trumpet-shaped blossom that eats insects.

Piping plover

WORDS TO KNOW

threatened *describing a species that is likely to become endangered in the foreseeable future*

endangered *describing a species in danger of becoming extinct*

the woods, while magnolias bloom white, pink, purple, yellow, or green depending on the species. About 80 types of magnolias grow in the state. The state tree is the palmetto, which has large, fanlike leaves and thrives in sandy soil along the coast.

Wildflowers dot woodlands, meadows, and swamps throughout the state. In the Blue Ridge, mountain laurel provides splashes of pink, while deep rose-colored blooms decorate the dark green leaves of the rhododendron. Yellow jessamine, the state flower, has small, pale yellow blooms. Other South Carolina wildflowers include cardinal flower, jack-in-the-pulpit, crane-fly orchid, spicebush, spiderwort, Solomon's seal, fire pink, and yellow passionflower.

ANIMAL LIFE

Different habitats in South Carolina attract different animal species. Swamps and rivers have plenty of fish, reptiles, and amphibians. Upstate forests have opossums, red foxes, and raccoons. Throughout the state, white-tailed deer browse on grasses and low-lying shrubs.

Reptiles and amphibians thrive in the state's mild climate. The largest reptile is the alligator, which is a threatened species in the state. South Carolina also has more than 40 species of snakes, including venomous species such as cottonmouths, copperheads, coral snakes, and three species of rattlesnakes. Salamanders, skinks, toads, and frogs join turtles and lizards in the swampy low country.

Red-tailed and red-shouldered hawks, swallow-tailed kites, bald eagles, falcons, and other birds of prey soar through the skies over South Carolina. Barred owls, barn owls, and great horned owls hunt small rodents at night. In the wetlands, herons, endangered wood storks, and

Two alligators emerge from the water onto a muddy riverbank.

egrets dip their bills into the water to catch small fish. Bird species range from tiny Carolina wrens to clumsy brown pelicans. There are colorful roseate spoonbills, brilliant red cardinals, and blue jays. One of the state's noisiest birds, the red-cockaded woodpecker, rat-a-tats in the old-growth pine forests in search of insects.

White-tailed deer are the most common large mammal. Black bears, bobcats, and eastern pumas (also called mountain lions) live in South Carolina as well.

PROTECTING THE ENVIRONMENT

South Carolina's population is growing rapidly. As more people move into the state, land that was once wild is being turned into housing, businesses, and schools. Wetlands, which clean water and act as a nursery for

South Carolina National Park Areas

This map shows some of South Carolina's national parks, monuments, preserves, and areas protected by the National Park Service.

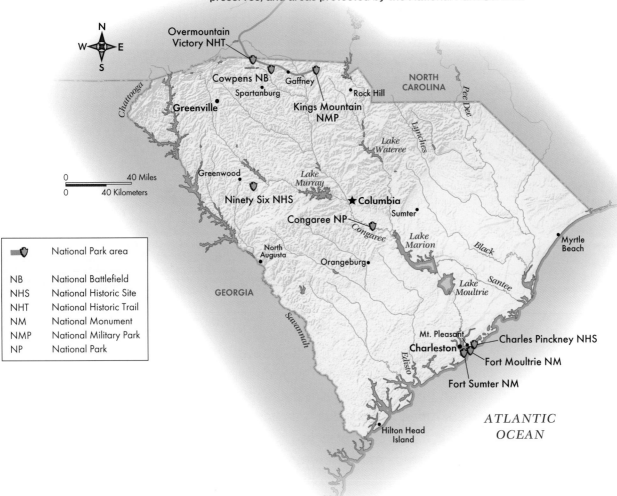

many fish species, are destroyed when they are filled in to create land for construction. The increasing number of people and roadways also puts native species at risk. From black bears and mountain lions in the hills to alligators and wood storks on the coast, many animals are losing habitat.

State programs such as the Heritage Trust have worked with organizations, including the Nature Conservancy, to preserve wild land and forests. The state has 20 wildlife refuges that protect a variety of habitats, including pine forests, open waters, ponds, and meadows. The Audubon Society has been active in protecting the state's endangered bird species. South Carolina is making an effort to restore its natural resources and conserve native animals and plants.

South Carolinians work to keep their natural areas clean and beautiful for everyone's use.

MINI-BIO

JAMES D. ELLIOTT JR.: CARING FOR BIRDS OF PREY

Over the years, real estate broker James D. Elliott Jr. saw many injured birds of prey in South Carolina. To help these birds, he founded the Charleston Raptor Center in 1991. In 1995, Elliott turned his hobby into a full-time career. Now the South Carolina Center for Birds of Prey, the raptor center has become one of the most highly regarded operations in the United States for saving and rehabilitating birds of prey. For his efforts, Elliott won the South Carolina Environmental Awareness Award in 2001.

? Want to know more?
See www.thecenterforbirdsofprey.org

READ ABOUT

Thousands of years ago, early inhabitants of the region hunted mammoths and other big game.

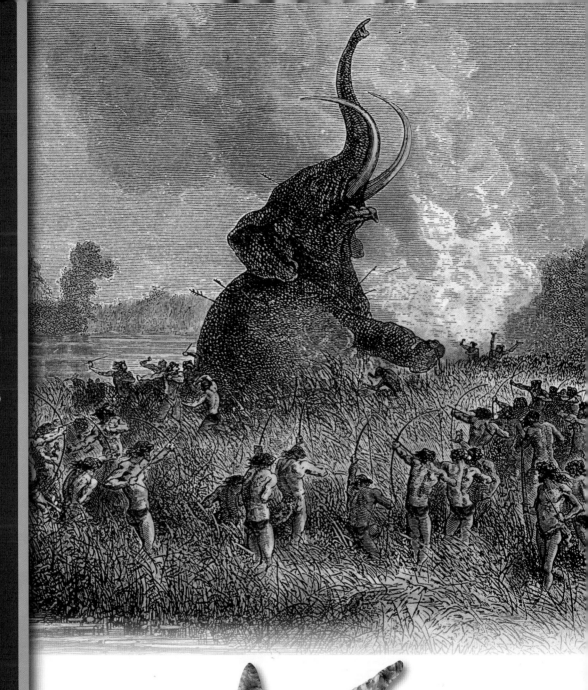

c. 11,000 BCE

Humans arrive in what is now South Carolina

▲ **c. 8000 BCE**

The Archaic culture develops

c. 2000 BCE

Native people build the Spanish Mount, a large mound made of shells

CHAPTER TWO

FIRST PEOPLE

★

PEOPLE FIRST ARRIVED IN PRESENT-DAY SOUTH CAROLINA IN SEARCH OF FOOD. Called Paleo-Indians, they were nomadic hunter-gatherers who moved from place to place, following herds of large animals such as mastodons and mammoths. Hunters worked together to capture a beast and kill it, using spears with stone spear points. Hunter-gatherers added to their diet by collecting ripe fruits, nuts, berries, and roots.

c. 1000 BCE
The Woodland culture develops

◀ **900 CE**
The Mississippian culture develops

1400s
Between 15,000 and 20,000 Native people live in what is now South Carolina

The earliest house found in South Carolina was built about 3,000 years ago. It was a small, D-shaped hut that could shelter a small group of people.

SEE IT HERE!

THE SPANISH MOUNT

The Spanish Mount is a mound built by Woodland people in what is now Edisto Beach State Park. The name itself is a puzzle, since the mound was built about 2000 BCE, 3,500 years before the Spanish visited the island. The Spanish Mount, which is made not of dirt but of shells, is in the shape of a large ring. It rests amid pines and palmettos. The mound is about 10 feet (3 m) high and 65 feet (20 m) long. How big was it when the Woodland people built it? Why did they build it? No one knows.

THE ARCHAIC CULTURE

Around 8000 BCE, mastodons and mammoths died off, perhaps because the climate had warmed. Hunters began focusing on smaller animals. This was the beginning of the Archaic period. Archaic people developed a device called an atlatl to help them throw spears harder and farther. With practice, hunters could bring down elk or deer. Archaic people also fished and collected clams, mussels, and crabs along the shore.

People began to build homes and establish small towns. These towns were usually temporary and moved with the seasons. Some important new skills were developed and changed people's lives. Archaic people made clay pottery bowls and jars, which allowed them to collect liquids and store foods.

THE WOODLAND CULTURE

The Woodland period lasted from 1000 BCE to about 900 CE. This was a time of great change for humans in South Carolina. The Woodland period saw the beginning of true farming. People went from collecting plant products (nuts, fruit, berries) that were growing in the wild to planting seeds of those plants where it was more convenient to have them grow. Improved skills in pottery and basket weaving allowed people to store more foods for winter use.

Because people needed to remain in one place to tend the crops, they built permanent villages. Groups moved with the seasons, but they spent the longest amount of time where they planted fields of grain, such as goosefoot and maygrass.

Woodland people began building large earthen mounds for ceremonial purposes. The group leader often lived in a building on top of the mound. A leader who died was buried on the site, and several more feet of dirt were added to the mound. Burial rituals became common, and many bodies were buried with household goods, tools, or ornaments.

THE MISSISSIPPIAN CULTURE

Between 900 and 1500 CE, the Woodland culture gave way to the Mississippian culture. The change from one culture to another was neither abrupt nor dramatic. During the Mississippian period, people developed a clearer social structure, with a definite chief, advisers, nobles, and workers.

The Mississippian people also built mounds. Their mounds were larger and more elaborate than those of the Woodland people. Mississippian mounds were usually in the shape of squat, flat-topped pyramids. Mississippians also built permanent cities, cleared large tracts of land for raising crops, and traveled to trade goods. Craftspeople began to use shells, stones, and copper for jewelry and decoration. These goods could be traded with distant cultures.

Corn, beans, and squash were the Mississippians' primary foods. These crops could be grown all in one field. Beans nourished the soil, growing tall by climbing

This shell gorget (a piece of armor worn over the throat) is from the Mississippian culture and dates to 1000 CE.

Native Americans from the Carolina region eat fruit while sitting on a mat made from rushes.

FAQ

Q8 WHAT WAS A FAVORITE FOOD OF SOUTH CAROLINA'S NATIVE PEOPLE?

A8 Nearly every Native woman learned how to cook a dish called *sofkee*. It was made by grinding and boiling dried corn. Sofkee is still eaten throughout the Southeast, but it is better known today as grits.

up cornstalks. Squash leaves spread out to keep down weeds and hold moisture in the soil. These foods could be preserved for later meals, and they provided ample seeds for the following year's crops.

NATIVE AMERICAN GROUPS

South Carolina's Native American nations emerged from the Mississippian culture. Some of these groups developed in what became South Carolina. Others moved into the area, forced to flee their homes by more power-

Native American Peoples

(Before European Contact)

This map shows the general area of Native American peoples before European settlers arrived.

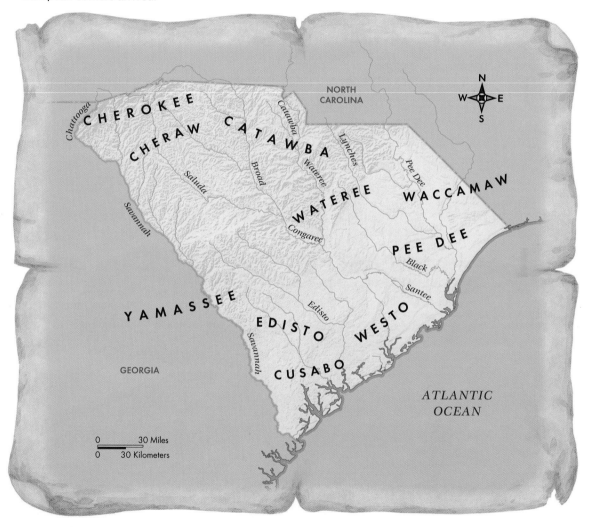

ful enemies. In the 1400s, between 15,000 and 20,000 Native people lived in what is now South Carolina.

South Carolina's many Native American societies included the Cherokee, Yamassee, Catawba, and Westo peoples. Most survived by hunting, fishing, and farming.

The principal crops were beans, corn, and squash, which were known as the Three Sisters. During long winter months, pots with these three key vegetables simmered over open fires and nourished hungry people.

The Cherokee People

Cherokees trace their heritage back more than 1,000 years. A typical Cherokee community consisted of up to 50 log houses surrounding a community square or council house. Homes were made by building a wooden frame that was covered with vines and branches and then coated with mud.

The Cherokee Nation was divided into seven clans, each with its own symbol. The clans were Bird, Paint,

The Cherokee people made baskets like these for storage.

Deer, Wolf, Blue, Long Hair, and Wild Potato. Membership in a clan was passed through the mother, so a child of a Wolf clan woman belonged to the Wolf clan.

Women played an important role in Cherokee life. Although men made the decisions for the nation as a whole, it was women who made decisions for their clans. Women helped feed the village by tilling the fields, gathering roots and nuts, and preserving food for the winter.

Raising children was an important job. Young girls needed to learn how to farm, cook, sew, and care for the sick. Boys had to learn how to hunt, fish, and protect the village. Many of the games Cherokee children played trained them for later life. Girls looked after dolls when they were young, and then younger brothers and sisters as they grew older. Boys needed to be skilled with bows and arrows for hunting. They participated in games to build their stamina for running and their strength for battling enemies. Both girls and boys helped their mothers with the farming and harvesting.

Cherokee traditional dress was practical and sturdy. Men wore leather **breechcloths** and leggings. In the summer, they went bare chested, while in winter, they added a fur robe for warmth. Men often shaved their heads, leaving only a single tuft of hair on top. They decorated themselves with tattoos on their faces or bodies. Women wore wraparound skirts and loose-fitting blouses that slipped over their heads. They wore their hair straight and long. Usually, a woman cut her hair only when she mourned the loss of a loved one.

Cherokees considered fire, which separates humans from other animals, to be a gift from the Great Spirit. During ceremonies, they would light the Sacred Fire, built only of oak and lit by a priest. The ritual lighting

WORD TO KNOW

breechcloths *garments worn by men over their lower bodies*

Picture Yourself...

at the Green Corn Festival

It is harvesttime. A full moon rises in the sky. In a few days, the hard work of gathering, husking, and preserving the corn will begin. Tonight, you will celebrate. The Green Corn Festival lasts several days, and this is your first year attending as a grown woman. This year, you **fasted** along with the other adults. You helped your grandmother, mother, and aunts clean your home, and you bathed to cleanse yourself. You drank the "black drink," a beverage made of herbs. After the fast, there will be work to do. You'll prepare corn soup from kernels shaved off the cob. Your aunt will make corn bread, while your mother will prepare a thick stew of deer meat and corn. Tonight begins the feast. There will be dancing, singing, and playing games. The Green Corn Festival is the most exciting time of the year.

WORD TO KNOW

fasted *went without eating*

A dance that may have been part of the Green Corn Festival

of the Sacred Fire was traditionally accompanied by feasting and dancing. Feasts, such as the Green Corn Festival, were also held to celebrate the planting and harvesting of corn.

The Westo People

The Westos once lived farther north, but the powerful Iroquois Nation had driven them out. They arrived in the Carolina region in the 1600s. They chose a plot of land near present-day Beaufort and soon came into

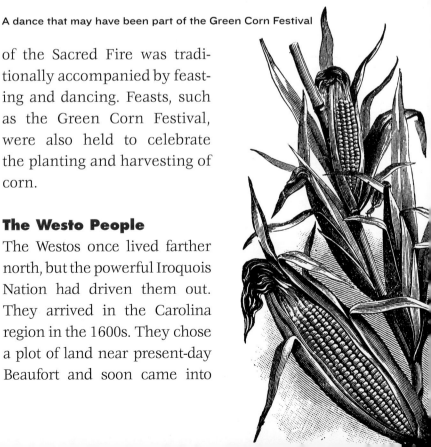

conflict with the Native Americans who already lived there. The Westos began making regular raids on other Native American nations and selling their captives into slavery.

The Edisto People

The Edisto people lived between the Savannah and Edisto rivers in villages with large, round houses in the center. The houses measured about 200 feet (61 m) in diameter and were constructed of sturdy limbs covered with palmetto fronds.

The Edisto chief was the official host when visitors came. Visitors came to the round house to speak with the chief, who sat on a throne above his people. Men, women, and children could attend the meeting and were seated on low benches around their chief.

The Catawba People

The Catawba people lived in what is now north-central South Carolina. Their name means "fork in a river," although the people called themselves *ye iswa,* or "river people." The Catawbas caught fish; farmed beans, corn, and squash; gathered nuts, berries, and roots; and hunted game. Men did the hunting and fishing and fought to protect the village. Women worked the fields, raised children, cooked, sewed, and nursed the wounded. Both men and women took part in telling stories and in producing art and music. Although most Catawba chiefs were men, there were several female chiefs.

Life seemed secure for the Native people of the region, but change was on the horizon. It was brought by newcomers who would soon arrive from across the ocean.

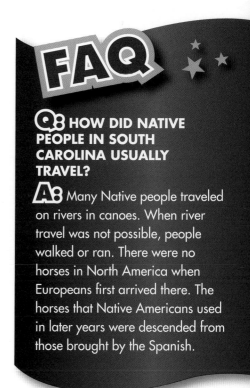

FAQ

Q8 HOW DID NATIVE PEOPLE IN SOUTH CAROLINA USUALLY TRAVEL?

A8 Many Native people traveled on rivers in canoes. When river travel was not possible, people walked or ran. There were no horses in North America when Europeans first arrived there. The horses that Native Americans used in later years were descended from those brought by the Spanish.

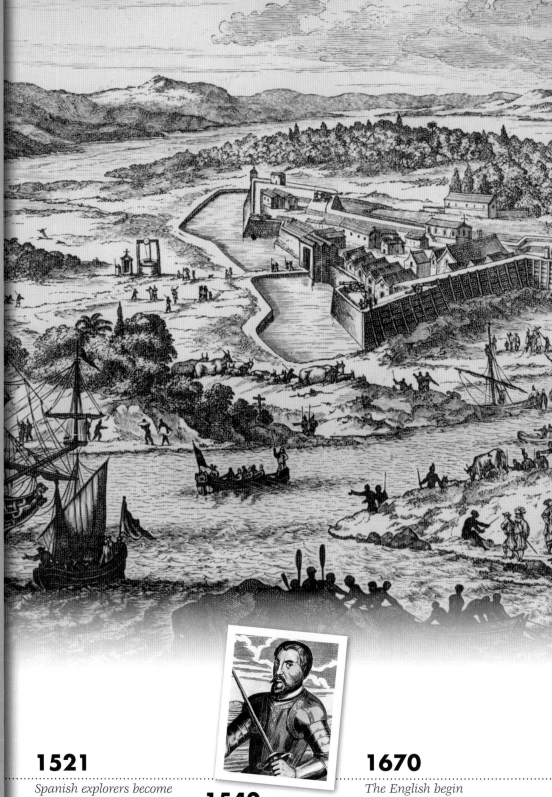

32

READ ABOUT

The settlement
of Charleston,
between the
Ashley and Cooper
rivers, in 1673

1521

*Spanish explorers become
the first Europeans to
land in what is now
South Carolina*

1540 ▲

*Spaniard Hernando de
Soto leads an expedition
into South Carolina*

1670

*The English begin
settling Carolina*

CHAPTER THREE

EXPLORATION AND SETTLEMENT

★

ESTABLISHING A SETTLEMENT IN SOUTH CAROLINA PROVED TO BE A STRUGGLE FOR EUROPEANS. The weather was hot and sticky during the summer, and the area endured hurricanes. The land was too swampy for planting, and the mosquitoes were awful. Several colonies failed before the British finally established a permanent colony in South Carolina in 1670.

1685 ▶
Rice is first brought to Carolina

1715
The Yamassee War begins

1739
Enslaved Africans take part in a revolt called the Stono Rebellion

Native Americans greeted Hernando de Soto and his crew when they came ashore in 1540.

EARLY EXPLORERS

The Spanish were the first Europeans to explore the coast of today's South Carolina. Although a Spanish ship passed by in 1514, the first recorded contact between the Spanish and Native people occurred in 1521. Lucas Vásquez de Ayllón, a wealthy planter from the Spanish colony on the island of Hispaniola in the Caribbean, sent two ships to investigate the coast that year. The Spanish captured and enslaved 70 Native Americans and brought them back to Hispaniola. In 1526, Vásquez de Ayllón sent 600 settlers, including many enslaved Africans, to form a colony on Carolina land, the first in what is now the United States. The colony struggled and then failed. The Spanish settlers had to abandon their new home within a few months. They left, but the Africans remained behind. They joined the local Native Americans, becoming the first people from abroad to live in a permanent settlement in what is now the United States.

European Exploration of South Carolina

The colored arrows on this map show the routes taken by explorers between 1522 and 1526.

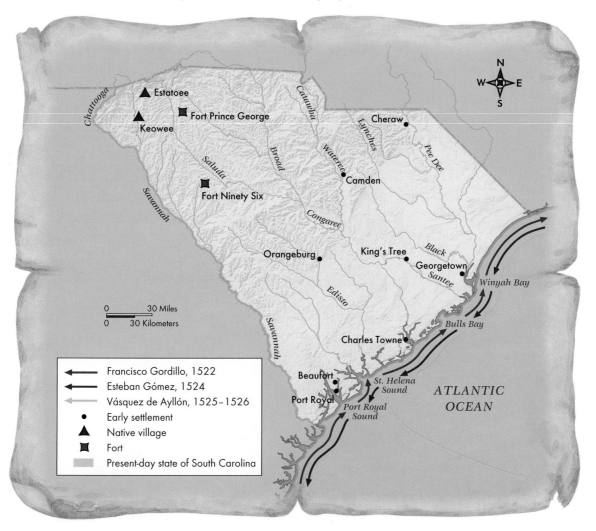

Francisco Gordillo, 1522
Esteban Gómez, 1524
Vásquez de Ayllón, 1525–1526
● Early settlement
▲ Native village
▪ Fort
Present-day state of South Carolina

In 1540, another Spaniard, Hernando de Soto, traveled through the Southeast. He ventured into present-day South Carolina in search of gold and gemstones but found none.

The next Europeans to arrive were a group of French Huguenots, Protestants who fled France in search of religious freedom. Captain Jean Ribault and his followers built Charlesfort on Parris Island in 1562. Ribault left 27 men in charge of protecting the settlement while he sailed back to France for supplies. Ribault did not return when he promised. Back in the settlement, the French grew restless. Instead of continuing to wait for Ribault, they built a boat and sailed for France themselves in 1563.

More than 60 years later, King Charles I of England granted the land between Virginia and Spanish Florida to Sir Robert Heath. This massive piece of land, called Carolana, stretched from the Atlantic to the Pacific. Despite having such a huge grant, Heath did nothing about setting up a colony. By 1663, the king's son, Charles II, was on the throne. He decided to give the land, by then called Carolina, to eight noblemen called the Lords Proprietors.

After Jean Ribault left them behind, these French settlers built a ship and sailed back to France.

THE GROWING COLONY

It took the Lords Proprietors nearly seven years to convince enough people to move before they could start their new colony. In October 1669, three ships left England with 92 brave settlers. Storms tossed the ships amid high seas. Many of the travelers became seasick. The food quickly went stale, and meals of **hardtack** and salt beef had little appeal.

None of the eight original Lords Proprietors ever crossed the Atlantic to Carolina. They chose a representative to act as governor but did not deal directly with their land grant. Anthony Ashley Cooper, the Earl of Shaftesbury, was the most involved of all the lords. Two South Carolina rivers, the Ashley and the Cooper, bear his name.

The lords placed advertisements to encourage settlers. Some colonists came to Carolina from England, others from Barbados. Some brought enslaved Africans with them. Over the next dozen years, more than 1,000 settlers arrived in Carolina. They worked as carpenters, farmers, bricklayers, shipping merchants, and smithies. The enslaved Africans tended fields and cattle. Some of the colonists also paid the travel expenses for European people who signed up to work as **indentured servants**.

RICE AND PIRATES

In 1685, a sea captain sent a gift of seed rice to Charleston as a thank-you gift for quick repair of his ship. The English had no skill at growing rice, but they quickly discovered that Africans—many

WORDS TO KNOW

hardtack *dried biscuits*

indentured servants *people who work for others under contract*

Picture Yourself . . .

as an Indentured Servant

To escape poverty, you have signed a contract as an indentured servant. You agree to work for the next seven years in exchange for transport to North America. For those seven years, you have no rights. You must work every day. In return, you get food, shelter, and one change of clothing each year. You may be beaten or abused, but you have no recourse. The contract holder owns you for the term of indenture. And if he says you violated the contract, then he can hold you for many years longer.

Enslaved workers loading rice onto barges in South Carolina

of whom had grown rice in their homeland—had the knowledge needed to make it a profitable crop. Wealthy colonists set up large farms, called plantations, by draining swampland in the region. The late 1600s saw rapid expansion of the Carolina Colony.

Rice made the wealthy colonists in Carolina even wealthier. As rice planters gained more wealth, they bought more land and needed more skilled Africans to grow the rice. Charleston became a central port for shipping rice to Europe and bringing in enslaved Africans. By the early 1700s, planters were exporting more than 300 tons of rice yearly to England and the West Indies. And by 1708, Africans made up a majority of South Carolina's population.

The colony's wealthy people attracted some unwanted attention, too: pirates! The Charleston shipping lanes attracted pirates such as Blackbeard, Stede

Bonnet, Christopher Moody, and Anne Bonny, one of several female pirates and a native of Charleston. Piracy struck fear in the hearts of ship captains sailing the South Carolina coast. The pirates seized ships and cargo and held well-to-do travelers for ransom. Pirates enjoyed two exceedingly profitable periods: 1670–1700 and 1716–1720. Most colonists lost some friends, family members, or personal goods to the pirates plaguing South Carolina.

THE YAMASSEE WAR

As more and more Europeans arrived in North America, Native Americans were forced off their land. The Edistos, Ashepoos, Stonos, and other small nations lost their land to Europeans and were preyed upon in slave raids. By the mid-1600s, the few surviving Edistos moved inland to join other, larger Native American groups. Meanwhile, the Westo people made a trade agreement with the European colonists in which they received goods in return for captured Native Americans or animal skins. Besides losing land to settlers, Native Americans also fought losing battles with European diseases. Smallpox, chicken pox, and measles wiped out many Native populations.

Although some Carolinians set up trading partnerships, such as buying furs from Native hunters, many

MINI-BIO

BLACKBEARD: LEGENDARY PIRATE

The waters off Charleston teemed with pirates when Blackbeard (1680?–1718) sailed the seas. Born Edward Teach, Blackbeard was rumored to wear a large black hat, swords at his waist, and knives and pistols across his chest. He learned the pirating trade under Captain Benjamin Hornigold and preyed on trading vessels traveling between Europe, the West Indies, and the North American colonies. Blackbeard's favorite ship was the Queen Anne's Revenge, a vessel he captured from the French.

 Want to know more? See www.ncmaritime.org/Blackbeard/default.htm

European settlers clashed with the Yamassee people in the Yamassee War of 1715.

CHEROKEE LEADER

Attakullakulla (c. 1700–c. 1780), a Cherokee leader and diplomat, tried to smooth out the problems between white settlers and Cherokees. In the 1750s, he negotiated with the South Carolina and Virginia colonies to try to increase trade. During the American Revolution, both the British troops and the American colonists tried to enlist the help of the Cherokees, but Attakullakulla refused to fight on either side.

believed that swindling the Indians out of their land was acceptable. In 1715, the Yamassee people, a mixture of Native Americans and Africans, had had enough. They began attacking English plantations. Other groups such as Cherokees, Creeks, and Choctaws joined the fight to save their land and ways of life. European settlers fled the countryside, hoping to find safety in Charleston.

For three years, Native Americans in Carolina fought the onslaught of white settlers. During that time, the Lords Proprietors sat safely in England and did little to help Carolinians.

In 1719, Carolinians rebelled against the Lords Proprietors. They asked Great Britain's king to declare the colony a crown colony and take over rule from the lords. This situation was resolved in 1729 when the crown purchased the proprietors' shares in Carolina and declared it a royal colony.

SLAVERY

Despite the conflict, Carolina planters continued to thrive. In 1715, enslaved Africans accounted for 60 percent of the Carolina population. Still, Carolina planters believed they needed more. From 1730 to 1739, slave traders brought 20,000 more enslaved Africans to Carolina. By 1740, enslaved Africans accounted for two-thirds of the colony's 59,000 people.

Enslaved people lived and worked in brutal conditions. They could legally be bought and sold, beaten, and even killed. Many enslaved people tried to run away, and those who were caught were punished severely. In 1739, in Stono, South Carolina, enslaved Africans captured firearms and planned to battle their way to Spanish Florida and freedom. Called the Stono Rebellion, this was the first large-scale revolt by enslaved Africans. White officials put down the revolt, and 60 of those who had fought for their liberty were executed.

Enslaved Africans lived in cabins like this one in Mount Pleasant.

The following year, South Carolina passed laws that imposed strict rules on the slaves. These slave codes prohibited enslaved people from traveling without written permission. Africans could not hold group meetings without a white person being present. They could not raise their own food, have money, or learn to read or write. They were also banned from owning or using drums, horns, or any other instrument that might be used to secretly communicate with other enslaved Africans.

Enslaved workers harvesting cotton on a plantation

By the middle of the 18th century, nine of the ten wealthiest people in the American colonies lived in South Carolina. All nine lived in the Charleston area and had grown rich running rice, cotton, or indigo plantations.

PROSPERITY

Rice grows in flooded fields, so South Carolina's swamps, where dikes could be built to control the flow of freshwater, were ideal as rice fields. But the dry areas farther inland were not. As more Carolinians moved inland, they needed crops that could be grown in the type of soil available. Two new crops became major moneymakers for South Carolina planters: cotton and indigo.

Colonists grew cotton and sent bales of it to England to be made into cloth. This was common for many colonial products. Raw materials—cotton, wool, timber, and furs—went to England to be turned into finished goods. Linens, towels, cloth and clothing, furniture, and fur-trimmed coats returned to the colonies to be sold in local shops.

In 1739, Eliza Lucas realized that cloth manufacturers would need a source for indigo, a plant used to dye cloth blue. So she began growing indigo. By 1745, she had married Charles Pinckney and expanded her indigo business dramatically. By 1747, indigo production in South Carolina was second only to rice as a cash crop, with more than 130,000 pounds (59,000 kilograms) of it exported through Charleston Harbor.

Indigo

THE ROAD TO REVOLUTION

Far to the north, European settlers had spread westward, moving into the Ohio Valley. In 1754, France and Great Britain went to war over control of this area and its rich fur trade. The conflict, called the French and Indian War, lasted from 1754 to 1763. Britain won the war.

At the war's end, Great Britain was dominant in North America. The British wanted to prevent the possibility of another war with the French, so they established an army in the colonies. An army costs a great deal of money, and the French and Indian War had already run Great Britain deeply into debt. The solution to Britain's financial woes was to tax the colonists whom the army was protecting. In the mid-18th century, many South Carolinians were prosperous and loyal to Great Britain. But as Great Britain began imposing taxes, South Carolinians and other colonists grew more discontented. The American colonies were on the road to revolution.

INDIGO ENTREPRENEUR

Botanist and **entrepreneur** Eliza Lucas Pinckney (1722–1793) introduced a new crop to the South Carolina colony—indigo. Pinckney realized that an abundance of cotton required more dyes to color the thread and cloth. She began planting and producing high-quality indigo. She became one of the most prominent people in the colony, and when she died, George Washington served as a pallbearer at her funeral.

WORD TO KNOW

entrepreneur *someone who manages and takes the risk of starting a business*

READ ABOUT

A Carolina colonist tries to beat away a British tax collector.

1776

Colonists win the Battle of Sullivan's Island, their first victory in the American Revolution

▲ **1788**

South Carolina becomes the eighth state

early 1800s

Cotton becomes South Carolina's major crop

CHAPTER FOUR

GROWTH AND CHANGE

★

I N 1764, THE BRITISH GOVERNMENT PASSED THE SUGAR ACT. It taxed sugar and molasses, items used daily. The next year, the Stamp Act was passed. It required a tax stamp on all printed documents—wills, contracts, bills of sale, newspapers, and even playing cards. Colonists were so angry over the Stamp Act that it was canceled.

1860
South Carolina is the first state to secede from the Union

1861
The Civil War begins at Fort Sumter

1868 ▶
Francis Cardozo is the first African American to hold statewide office in the United States

FROM TAXES TO WAR

The British replaced the Stamp Act with the Townshend Acts in 1767. These acts charged duties, or fees, on imports of lead, glass, paper, and tea. As a major trade port, Charleston was hard-hit by import duties. Many Charleston citizens found a way around the taxes—they smuggled goods past the customs officers.

Some colonists were particularly angry about the taxes because they could not vote for representatives in Parliament, the British lawmaking body. They did not think it was fair to be taxed without anyone speaking on their behalf and cried, "No taxation without representation." The colonists decided to create their own Congress.

In 1774, South Carolina sent Christopher Gadsden, Thomas Lynch Jr., Henry Middleton, John Rutledge, and Edward Rutledge as representatives to the First Continental Congress. The Congress drafted a list of complaints to send to Great Britain's King George III. The king was not interested.

The next year, the American Revolution began with the Battles of Lexington and Concord in Massachusetts. Shortly thereafter, the Second Continental Congress met. Congress chose George Washington to lead the Continental army.

Early on, the American Revolution did not go well for the colonists. Great Britain had an experienced, trained, well-supplied army, while the Continental army was made up of farmers, trappers, blacksmiths, teachers, and others with little military experience.

Picture Yourself . . .

at the Second Continental Congress
It is late June 1776, and it's hot, sticky, and miserable in Carpenters' Hall in Philadelphia, Pennsylvania. Tempers flare during the meetings of the Second Continental Congress. You represent South Carolina, and you know that many South Carolinians want freedom from Great Britain. Virginia delegate Thomas Jefferson reads a draft of a document that he calls a Declaration of Independence: "We hold these truths to be self-evident, that all men are created equal." The draft passes, and the document is copied, ready for signing. You take a quill pen in your hand and dip the point in the inkwell. With a slight hesitation, you sign your name, committing the colonists of South Carolina to a path from which there can be no return.

Soldiers at Fort Moultrie battled British forces on June 28, 1776.

In 1775, when the war began, South Carolina's royal governor, William Campbell, fled Charleston. The following year, South Carolina set up an independent state government, with John Rutledge as the head of the Congress. South Carolinians were divided. Patriots wanted independence from Britain; Loyalists hoped to restore ties to what they considered their mother country.

The fighting in South Carolina began on June 28, 1776. The British attacked Fort Moultrie, a ramshackle fort built of palmetto logs on Sullivan's Island, near Charleston. The battle lasted nine and a half hours and was the colonists' first decisive victory over the British navy during the Revolution.

In 1780, the British laid siege to Charleston for two months. They blockaded ships from entering the port and bombarded the city. Charleston fell to the British, who then marched through South Carolina with ease. In August 1780, the British defeated the Continental troops at Camden. During that time, American victories in South Carolina were limited to minor skirmishes by Francis Marion and his forces, which included both black and white soldiers. Marion used **guerrilla** tactics to

The palmetto is South Carolina's state tree because palmetto logs were the building material at Fort Moultrie, the site of the American colonists' first victory in the Revolution.

WORD TO KNOW

guerrilla *describing soldiers who don't belong to regular armies; they often use surprise attacks and other uncommon battle tactics*

South Carolina: From Colony to Statehood

(1663–1788)

This map shows the original South Carolina colony and the area (in yellow) that became the state of South Carolina in 1788.

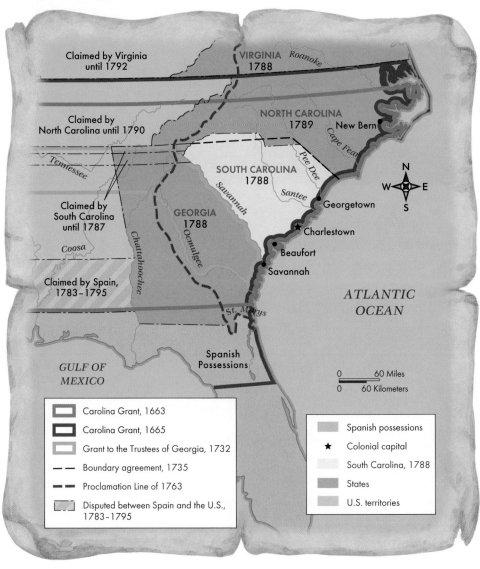

Claimed by Virginia until 1792

VIRGINIA 1788

Roanoke

Claimed by North Carolina until 1790

NORTH CAROLINA 1789

New Bern

Tennessee

Cape Fear

SOUTH CAROLINA 1788

Pee Dee

Claimed by South Carolina until 1787

Savannah

Santee

N
W   E
S

Georgetown

Coosa

Chattahoochee

GEORGIA 1788

Ocmulgee

Charlestown

Beaufort

Savannah

Claimed by Spain, 1783–1795

St. Marys

ATLANTIC OCEAN

GULF OF MEXICO

Spanish Possessions

0   60 Miles
0   60 Kilometers

Carolina Grant, 1663
Carolina Grant, 1665
Grant to the Trustees of Georgia, 1732
Boundary agreement, 1735
Proclamation Line of 1763
Disputed between Spain and the U.S., 1783–1795

Spanish possessions
★   Colonial capital
South Carolina, 1788
States
U.S. territories

strike at British troops and supplies. An effort to reclaim South Carolina pitted Generals Nathanael Greene, Andrew Pickens, Thomas Sumter, and Francis Marion against larger, more powerful British forces. Slowly, the Americans forced the British back to Charleston.

In the western part of the state, Continental troops faced British troops at Kings Mountain and Cowpens. American victories at both sites helped secure the area against British advances. American troops pushed the British back toward the coast. In December 1782, the British left Charleston, and the following year, American and British officials signed a peace treaty. The United States was now an independent nation. In 1788, South Carolina approved the U.S. Constitution, becoming the eighth state.

American troops defeated the British at the Battle of Cowpens in January 1781.

MINI-BIO

FRANCIS MARION: THE SWAMP FOX

Called the Swamp Fox, Francis Marion (1732–1795) was a hero of the American Revolution. He and his men stole supplies, eluded capture by the Loyalists, and slipped back into the swamps of the low country without detection. Marion was a master of guerrilla war tactics, often attacking troops much larger than his band of patriots. By the end of the American Revolution, he had achieved the rank of general in the Continental army.

? **Want to know more?** See www.scstatehouse. net/studentpage/marion.htm

A HEROINE IN ACTION

Margaret Catherine Moore Barry (1752–1823) was a young wife when the American Revolution broke out. She was married to a man who became an officer in the Patriot forces. Barry herself served as a scout and a messenger. Her ride to warn the Patriots of the British arrival in Cowpens helped colonial troops prepare for the battle. She has been honored as a hero of the American Revolution.

A BOOMING ECONOMY

Throughout the late 1700s and early 1800s, South Carolina's economy thrived. Cotton plantations sprang up across the state. In 1793, Eli Whitney invented the cotton gin, a machine that separated cotton fibers from the sticky seeds. Processing cotton became much easier and more profitable, and cotton soon overtook rice and indigo as South Carolina's primary cash crop.

Cotton helped bring together the different parts of South Carolina. Before cotton became the "king" of crops, the uplands and the low country had little in common. Once cotton began to be grown throughout the state, everyone became concerned with the price of cotton, ways of harvesting and processing the fiber, and means of shipping. Roads crisscrossed the state, allowing inland farmers to haul their crop to Charleston for shipping overseas.

REBELLION

By the beginning of the 19th century, South Carolina had 196,000 white citizens, 146,000 enslaved Africans, and 3,200 free Africans. Most enslaved people worked cotton fields. By 1810, another 40,000 enslaved Africans would be added to the state's population.

Plantation owners believed slavery to be the most profitable means of growing crops. In the early 1800s, enslaved Africans protested the oppression of slavery through a series of rebellions and plots. The first rebellion occurred in 1810 in Camden, when a group of enslaved Africans tried to revolt against their owners. The rebellion was quickly put down, but the desire

Field-workers at the Hopkinson
Plantation in Charleston County, 1862

for freedom did not end. Twelve years later, Denmark Vesey, a minister and former slave, planned another rebellion that involved about a thousand people. Two servants told their masters about the planned revolt, and Vesey and many of his followers were arrested. Vesey and 33 other rebels were hanged for their efforts to attain freedom.

Enslaved people also rebelled in other ways. They pretended to be sick or injured so they could not work. Many ran away, following the Underground Railroad to freedom in the North or heading south to Florida. The Underground Railroad was a series of places where those fleeing slavery could find food, shelter, and help in their escape. Plantation owners were angry that people were helping enslaved Africans escape. Proslavery politicians proposed a remedy—the Fugitive Slave Act of 1850.

MINI-BIO

SARAH GRIMKE AND ANGELINA GRIMKE WELD: SPEAKING OUT

Sarah Grimke (1792–1873), shown here, and her sister Angelina Grimke Weld (1805–1879) were born on a South Carolina plantation to a prominent slave-holding family. The Grimke sisters became appalled at the injustice of slavery they saw every day. In 1838, Angelina became the first woman to speak to the Massachusetts state legislature about women's rights and ending slavery. Sarah was one of the first to compare the plight of women with that of enslaved people, saying a "woman has no political existence. . . . She is only counted like slaves in the south to swell the number of lawmakers."

 Want to know more? See www.greatwomen.org/women.php?action=viewone&id=70

The Fugitive Slave Act allowed slave owners to employ slave catchers to arrest people who had escaped slavery and made it to northern states. The slave catchers could arrest any African person and transport him or her to the South. Some of those who were arrested were actually free blacks, not people who had escaped slavery, but they had no way to protect themselves. Since they did not get a fair trial, they could not prove who they were; few judges would listen.

SECESSION AND THE CIVIL WAR

By the 1850s, the issue of slavery was threatening to tear the nation apart. Some Northerners wanted to abolish, or end, slavery entirely. Many more wanted to halt its expansion into new American territories in the West. But the labor of enslaved Africans had made some Southerners wealthy. They wanted to preserve slavery. They also believed that the federal government did not have the right to tell states whether they could have slavery.

In 1860, Abraham Lincoln was elected president of the United States. Some Southerners feared he would abolish slavery. Politicians in South Carolina held a convention to discuss what they should do. They decided to secede, or withdraw, from the Union. Other Southern states joined South Carolina in seceding. They formed the Confederate States of America and chose Jefferson Davis as their president. President Lincoln was ready to fight to preserve the Union. The nation was on the brink of civil war.

On April 12, 1861, Confederate troops fired on Union troops stationed at Fort Sumter in Charleston Harbor. The shots announced the beginning of the Civil War. After 34 hours of being bombarded, the fort surrendered. The first battle was over, and the South had won.

Many South Carolina men volunteered for the Confederate army and navy. Women prepared for war by storing food, making uniforms, and collecting

The battle at Fort Sumter in April 1861 marked the beginning of the Civil War.

SEE IT HERE!

FORT SUMTER

The first shots of the Civil War were fired at Fort Sumter. The fort sits on an island at the opening to Charleston Harbor. Today, you can explore the island and view its cannons, powder magazines, and the best collection of seacoast artillery in the United States. Fort Sumter National Monument gives visitors a fuller understanding of the events leading up to the Civil War.

The First South Carolina Volunteers take the oath of allegiance before entering the Union army.

Some African Americans who had been freed from slavery on the Sea Islands formed the First South Carolina Volunteers. They were the first black troops to battle the Confederacy.

medicines. Initially, many Southerners believed troops would march to war and return victorious in only a few months. No one was prepared for four years of war and the destruction that would leave 620,000 dead and more than 1 million wounded.

After the Union lost Fort Sumter, it began a blockade to prevent ships from bringing supplies into the city. Eleven warships prowled the coast in search of blockade-runners, quick ships that tried to slip past the blockade. South Carolina depended on exporting cotton and importing cloth, medicines, foods, and other necessities. Although blockade-runners were often successful at bringing goods through the Union line, the amount of trade was reduced to a fraction of what it had been before the war. Stores were empty, and food became scarce and expensive.

UNDERWATER WARFARE

The Confederate navy tried to end the Union blockade with an unusual ship—the *H. L. Hunley*. The *Hunley* was a human-powered submarine with a crew of eight and a torpedo stuck to its bow. After many disastrous trials in which the submarine sank, the *Hunley* was ready for action. In 1864, on its first mission, the *Hunley* attacked and sank the Union ship *Housatonic*, but the *Hunley* also sank. The submarine was raised from the mud outside Charleston Harbor on August 8, 2000, having been lost 136 years earlier.

By 1864, the Civil War had taken a new turn. The South had suffered serious defeats in Gettysburg, Pennsylvania, and Vicksburg, Mississippi. Ships no longer slipped through the blockaded seaports, and the people of the South were starving. Plantations that once burst with cotton began growing grain and vegetables. Africans left in droves as Union forces approached.

In 1864, Union general William T. Sherman and his troops marched north through Georgia, destroying railroad tracks and plantations and trying to wreck the South's will to fight. They then headed into South Carolina. In February 1865, much of Columbia burned. Historians are still not sure who actually set the fires, but after two days of fires, 458 city buildings and houses had been ruined.

MINI-BIO

ROBERT SMALLS: CIVIL WAR HERO

Robert Smalls (1839–1915) was born into slavery in Beaufort, South Carolina. Early in the Civil War, Smalls was working on the *Planter*, a Confederate ship that transported explosives and other goods. One night, he and other enslaved crew members took control of the ship, picked up their families from shore, and sailed past Confederate forts to the nearest Union ship, delivering the Confederate ship into Union hands. Smalls then commanded a ship in the Union army. After the war, he was elected to Congress.

? **Want to know more?** See www.robertsmalls.org/about.htm

WOW

On June 2, 1863, Harriet Tubman, who had been born into slavery, led Union troops in a Hilton Head raid that liberated 800 men, women, and children from slavery.

On February 18, 1865, the 55th Massachusetts Regiment, which was made up of African American soldiers, liberated Charleston from Confederate control. Their white commander, Charles Fox, described the scene as one in which the black residents turned out with "cheers, blessings, prayers, and songs . . . heard on every side." He continued, "The glory and triumph of this hour . . . can never be described. It was one of those occasions which happened but once in a lifetime, to be lived over in memory forever."

RECONSTRUCTION

The Civil War ended when Confederate general Robert E. Lee surrendered on April 9, 1865. A few days later, President Lincoln was assassinated. The nation faced the daunting task of rebuilding the South and bringing the Southern states back into the Union. This process, called Reconstruction, lasted from 1865 to 1877.

South Carolina planters, hoping to resume their hold over the state and its newly freed African Americans, passed a series of Black Codes in December 1865. These laws forbade free travel by African Americans and restricted the types of work African Americans could do. The laws also gave African Americans no political or economic rights. The state's military governor, who had been appointed by the federal government, rejected the Black Codes.

In 1867, the U.S. Congress ordered new constitutional conventions that would restore democracy to the southern states. African American voters, a majority in South Carolina, sent 76 black delegates to the convention. Together with 48 white delegates, they wrote the most democratic document in the state's history. It granted voting rights to all men, not just those with

Students listen to an instructor at the Zion School for Colored Children in Charleston, 1866.

property. It also created the state's first public school system, lowered taxes on the poor, increased services for the poor, established more hospitals, and abolished imprisonment for debt.

The new government created by the state's poor white and black voters also extended rights to women. Women had previously faced severe limitations on their rights to own property, to have legal access to divorce, and to win custody of their children in divorce proceedings. But South Carolina's new, more democratic government still did not grant women the right to vote.

South Carolina's new leaders, both black and white, took over a government deeply in debt. They tried mightily to set the state on a road to a better future, and for a number of years, life improved for residents of all backgrounds.

MINI-BIO

JONATHAN J. WRIGHT: FIGHTING FOR JUSTICE

Jonathan J. Wright (1840–1885) was born and educated in Pennsylvania, moved to South Carolina, organized schools for African Americans, and was elected to the state senate. Twice elected to the state supreme court, he served for seven years, with the distinction of being the first African American elected to any state's highest judicial post. While serving on the South Carolina Supreme Court, Wright was forced to leave a railroad car reserved for white passengers. He sued the railroad and won $1,200 in damages. Following the takeover of the state government by white supremacists in 1876, he resigned.

? **Want to know more?** See www.blackpast.org/ ?q=aah/wright-jonathan-j-1840-1885

During this period, South Carolinians elected many African Americans to high office, including eight congressmen, two lieutenant governors, two attorneys general, and a justice of the state supreme court. Francis Cardozo was elected secretary of state in 1868, making him the first African American to hold statewide office in the United States. He later became state treasurer.

In the aftermath of the Civil War, a violent, racist group called the Ku Klux Klan (KKK) had been founded in Tennessee. Klan groups soon spread across the country. By the early 1870s, the Klan had been suppressed in South Carolina. But a mur-

This group of men served in Congress during the 1870s. Among them are three South Carolinians: Joseph H. Rainey and Robert Brown Elliott (seated, far right) and Robert C. DeLarge (standing, left).

African American workers loading cotton bales, 1878

derous group called the Red Shirts became involved in Klan-like violence. In 1876, South Carolina's Reconstruction government fell in the face of this violence, which was supported by politicians and planters who had fought to keep slavery. Once again, the wealthy whites ruled the state.

WORD TO KNOW

civil rights *basic human rights that all citizens in a society are entitled to, such as the right to vote*

MINI-BIO

ROBERT B. ELLIOTT: U.S. REPRESENTATIVE

Robert Brown Elliott (1842–1884) served South Carolina as a member of the U.S. House of Representatives. Born and educated in England, Elliott moved to South Carolina and worked as a lawyer. He served at the South Carolina constitutional convention after the Civil War and became a member of the state house of representatives in 1868. Two terms in the U.S. Congress followed, during which he fought for the passage of a civil rights act. Later, he was again elected to the state legislature, serving as speaker of the house.

Want to know more? See http://bioguide. congress.gov/scripts/biodisplay.pl?index=E000128

READ ABOUT

Charleston hosts a carnival in 1926.

1895

South Carolina writes a new constitution that allows segregation

1910–1940

About 250,000 African Americans leave South Carolina during the Great Migration

◄**1920s**

A boll weevil infestation devastates the state's cotton industry

CHAPTER FIVE

MORE MODERN TIMES

★

A S THE 20TH CENTURY STARTED, SOUTH CAROLINA FOUND ITSELF AT A CROSSROADS. Some people were looking toward the future, hoping to improve their lives and change society. Others wanted to return to the past, to the way things had once been. Those two groups of people would soon be in conflict.

1963
Harvey Gantt becomes the first African American admitted to Clemson University

1999 ▸
Civil rights groups begin a boycott to attempt to force South Carolina to stop flying the Confederate flag

2000–2007
South Carolina loses 5,000 textile jobs

African American workers at a printing press in Orangeburg

WORDS TO KNOW

segregation *separation from others, according to race, class, ethnic group, religion, or other factors*

textile *cloth or fabric that is woven, knitted, or otherwise manufactured*

SEGREGATION AND SHARECROPPING

Based on the 1895 state constitution and a U.S. Supreme Court decision called *Plessy v. Ferguson*, the state was allowed to offer "separate but equal" facilities to black and white citizens. This meant that the state could force African Americans to attend separate schools or use separate hospitals, as long as those institutions were considered "equal" to those offered for white citizens. In practice, that equality was seldom real.

Segregation became the law in South Carolina. African Americans had to drink from separate water fountains and use separate restrooms. They could not eat in the same restaurants as whites or work side by side with whites. In **textile** mills, African Americans worked in separate rooms from whites. In Columbia, African Americans had to ride in separate streetcars. In Charleston, they could not swim at Folly Beach, the Isle of Palms, or Sullivan's Island. Most African Americans were also prevented from voting.

In the years after the Civil War, southern landowners had replaced slavery with sharecropping. Under the sharecropping system, a landowner and a sharecropper signed a contract. The landowner provided the land; advanced money for seeds, tools, and food; and arranged for the sale of cotton or tobacco after the harvest. The sharecropper did the work and took all the risk. The fee for land rental was usually half the crop. If the crop was poor, the farmer still owed the rental fee.

Landowners charged high rates for loaning money, which also was paid by portions of the harvested crop. Frequently, a sharecropping family worked all year only to find out that the crop did not cover their debts. Each year drove sharecroppers, both black and white, deeper into debt, while rich landowners grew even richer. Sharecropping made growing cotton even more profitable for landowners than it had been under slavery.

A sharecropping family

THE GREAT MIGRATION AND WORLD WAR I

Beginning in about 1910, large numbers of African Americans began leaving the South to start new lives in the North. Many saw no hope for success in the South. They could earn far more money working in a northern factory than they could back home in the southern states. During this period, called the Great Migration, South Carolina's population changed. For most of the previous 200 years, African Americans had composed the majority of the state's population. So many African Americans left the state that by 1930, whites had become the majority. Some 250,000 African Americans left the state during this period.

When World War I (1914–1918) began in Europe, the United States did not immediately join the war. However, U.S. factories geared up to provide supplies to European allies. The U.S military also began preparing for war. Greenville, Spartanburg, and Columbia, South Carolina, worked to get army training centers in their cities. As more northerners joined the military, still more African Americans fled the South for newly available jobs in northern factories.

In 1917, the United States officially entered the war. South Carolina's two major industries—textiles and agriculture—flourished as the needs of the military increased. The value of textile production in the state increased from $168 million in 1916 to $326 million in 1918, while the value of agricultural production rose from $121 million in 1916 to $446 million two years later.

More than 65,000 South Carolinians, both black and white, served in the military during the war. Meanwhile, families back in South Carolina planted "liberty gardens" to add to their food supply. Some families had "wheatless" or "meatless" days because grain and meat were **rationed**.

THE GREAT DEPRESSION

South Carolina's prosperity did not continue for long after World War I ended. By the 1920s, the cotton industry was devastated by an insect called the boll weevil. Boll weevils could destroy an entire cotton crop. They laid eggs in the plant; their **larvae** grew by eating the cotton inside the boll. For sharecroppers, the boll weevil was the worst possible disaster because many landowners insisted that sharecroppers grow only cotton.

South Carolina soon faced even worse economic troubles. In 1929, the Great Depression began. All across the nation, banks and factories went out of business, and people lost their life savings. As businesses closed, people were thrown out of work. In 17 South Carolina counties, one in three workers was unemployed. People

WORDS TO KNOW

rationed *controlled the amount one could use*

larvae *newly hatched young of an animal that look very different from the adult*

Civilian Conservation Corps workers plant pine seeds in Georgetown, late 1930s.

had no money to buy food for their families or pay the mortgage on their houses, and many people lost their homes. The Depression was a time of great suffering.

Relief came when Franklin D. Roosevelt became president in 1933 and introduced his New Deal, a series of programs designed to put Americans back to work. South Carolina's Mary McLeod Bethune, an African American educator, advised Roosevelt as the director of Negro Affairs for the National Youth Administration.

Under the New Deal, the Works Progress Administration (WPA) put South Carolinians back to work building schools, libraries, and bridges. WPA writers interviewed hundreds of Carolinians and recorded oral histories of the state. Artists produced murals and sculptures for post offices and other public buildings around the state. The Civilian Conservation Corps (CCC) planted trees and developed state parks.

W★W

By June 1942, nearly 50,000 men had worked on South Carolina CCC projects. They built nearly 900 bridges, 129 lookout towers, and 16 state parks, and planted more than 56 million trees.

66

MINI-BIO

MARY McLEOD BETHUNE: LIFELONG EDUCATOR

Mary McLeod Bethune (1875–1955) was born in Mayesville in central South Carolina to parents who had been enslaved until the Civil War. She was one of 17 children. Bethune showed an early desire to read and write, and she grew up to become a teacher. In 1904, she founded the Daytona Normal and Industrial Institute for Negro Girls, now known as Bethune-Cookman University in Florida. She became a close friend of first lady Eleanor Roosevelt and advised President Franklin Roosevelt on issues relating to the African American community. Bethune served as director of Negro Affairs for the National Youth Administration from 1936 to 1944, helping young African Americans get jobs in their communities.

? Want to know more? See www.greatwomen.org/women.php?action=viewone&id=18

Even with the federal government employing millions of workers, the Great Depression did not end. The country would not pull out of the Depression until World War II began in Europe in 1939.

WORLD WAR II

Although the United States tried to stay out of the war, President Roosevelt agreed to sell war supplies to Great Britain, France, and the countries that were fighting Germany in Europe. Suddenly, U.S. factories that had been closed for years opened for business 24 hours a day. In South Carolina, textile factories churned out miles of cloth to be used for uniforms, tents, duffel bags, and bandages. Farmers planted their fields with cotton, tobacco, and food crops. And many more African Americans from South Carolina left the state to work at factories producing war goods in northern states.

In 1941, the United States entered World War II after Japan attacked the U.S. naval base at Pearl Harbor, Hawai'i. Thousands of South Carolinians joined the military, while those at home kept homes and factories working. Women who had never worked outside the home became electricians, plumbers, textile workers, riveters, and shipbuilders—and found they enjoyed working and earning paychecks. At least 900,000 men trained for the military at camps in South Carolina.

A member of the Women's Army Auxiliary Corps at the Fort Jackson military base, December 1943

Some 180,000 Carolinians, including 2,500 women, entered the military. At home, tires, gas, and food such as sugar, meat, and coffee were rationed so that there would be enough supplies for the military.

THE CIVIL RIGHTS MOVEMENT

African American men and women had joined the military, fought in the war, and enjoyed freedoms they did not have at home in South Carolina. Like the women who had taken factory jobs, they did not want to return to life as it was before the war. They resented living under the restrictions of segregation. Even though they had fought for their country, they could not enjoy the same freedoms as other Americans. But soon, a civil rights movement emerged that would shake the state and the South for the next 25 years and beyond.

A class at the St. Anne School in Rock Hill, one of the few integrated schools in South Carolina, 1957

WORD TO KNOW

desegregate *to end the practice of keeping races separate from each other in education or other community activities*

In 1947, African American Levi Pearson filed a petition with the Clarendon County public schools requesting transportation to school for his three children. White children in the district already had bus transportation, but black children did not. Eventually this case, which was called *Briggs v. Elliott,* joined *Brown v. Board of Education,* a case that challenged school segregation in Kansas. In 1954, the U.S. Supreme Court heard the joined case and determined that the policy of "separate but equal" was illegal. School districts in the South were ordered to **desegregate**.

The South Carolina government tried to prevent desegregating schools, but its efforts failed. In 1963, Harvey Gantt became the first African American to attend Clemson, one of the state's leading universities.

A year later, after enormous pressure from African American men and women, the federal government passed the Civil Rights Act, followed the next year by the Voting Rights Act. The Civil Rights Act banned segregation in public facilities. The Voting Rights Act outlawed voting restrictions that discriminated against African Americans. By 1965, almost 40 percent of African Americans in the state had registered to vote.

Although Gantt's attendance at Clemson went smoothly, it was not so easy for many African American students at other schools throughout the South. In 1968, students from the South Carolina State University campus at Orangeburg protested against a "whites only" bowling alley. Highway patrol officers arrived and shot into the crowd, wounding 28 protesters and killing three others.

Two years later, the most violent act of the civil rights era in South Carolina took place in Lamar. Between 150 and 200 white men and women attacked a school bus carrying African American students to a previously all-white high school. The attackers clashed with highway patrolmen and other law enforcement officials. The day after the riot, the state National Guard was at the school to keep the peace.

Throughout the rest of the 1900s, African Americans made significant advances in South Carolina. Two Carolinians became National Aeronautics and Space Administration astronauts—Charles Bolden and Ronald McNair. North Charleston native Art Shell was the first African American to become a head coach in the National Football League. James Clyburn became the first South Carolina African American elected to the U.S. Congress since the late 1800s. Schooling, better jobs, and political positions began to open to people of color, providing opportunities for African Americans to succeed in South Carolina.

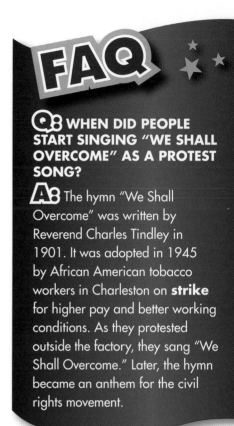

FAQ

Q8 WHEN DID PEOPLE START SINGING "WE SHALL OVERCOME" AS A PROTEST SONG?

A8 The hymn "We Shall Overcome" was written by Reverend Charles Tindley in 1901. It was adopted in 1945 by African American tobacco workers in Charleston on **strike** for higher pay and better working conditions. As they protested outside the factory, they sang "We Shall Overcome." Later, the hymn became an anthem for the civil rights movement.

WORD TO KNOW

strike *an organized refusal to work, usually as a sign of protest about working conditions*

MINI-BIO

SEPTIMA POINSETTE CLARK: ACTIVIST AND EDUCATOR

Septima Poinsette Clark (1898–1987) was an African American educator, civil rights leader, and humanitarian. As a young woman, Clark became a teacher and school principal. She soon began working to see that African American teachers received the same pay as white teachers. She later began a program to teach adults to read and fill out documents such as voter registration forms and other applications. Her Citizenship Schools were established throughout the South. For her lifelong efforts to ensure racial equality, Clark has been called the Queen Mother of the American Civil Rights Movement.

? Want to know more? See www.usca.edu/aasc/Clark.htm

WORD TO KNOW

boycott *the organized refusal to use a service or buy a product, as a form of protest*

RECENT TIMES

While African Americans fought for equality, so did women. State taxes had long supported the Citadel, an all-male military college. In 1995, Shannon Faulkner became the first woman to enter the school, after suing for admission on the basis that single-sex education at a state-funded school was unconstitutional. Although Faulkner did not graduate from the Citadel, her efforts opened the door for other young women. By 2005, 118 female cadets were attending the school.

Two major issues followed South Carolinians into the 21st century: the flying of the Confederate flag above the State House and the failing textile industry. Both issues have had a major impact on South Carolina's economy.

In 1962, South Carolina legislators were angry about having to end segregation, so they began flying the Confederate battle flag over the state capitol. Through the years, the flag continued to fly over the capitol, despite the objections of many South Carolinians. In 1999, civil rights organizations began a **boycott** of South Carolina tourism sites. Since that time, more than 100 conventions and business groups have supported the boycott. This has hurt South Carolina's multibillion-dollar tourism industry. In April 2000, the state senate gave in—but not completely. Lawmakers agreed to move the Confederate flag from the top of the capitol to a monument for Confederate soldiers. Many people were not satisfied with this move, and the boycott remains in effect.

In recent years, the state's largest industry struggled for survival. In 1994, the United States entered into the North American Free Trade Agreement (NAFTA). NAFTA made it cheaper to manufacture textile products in Mexico than in the United States. About 5,000 textile jobs were eliminated in South Carolina between 2000 and 2007, when companies moved their plants to countries such as China, Taiwan, and Mexico. Today, the South Carolina government is attracting other industries to fill the job gap. Anderson County, for example, has lost textile mills but has become a center for the manufacture of plastics, automotive parts, and other machinery. Meanwhile, colleges are retraining workers so they will be skilled for jobs needed in the 21st century. These are steps toward providing South Carolina with a bright economic future.

The 2008 Martin Luther King Day rally was held on the State House grounds, near the spot where the Confederate flag now flies.

READ ABOUT

A kayaker in the
marshlands near
Charleston

CHAPTER SIX

PEOLE

★

SOUTH CAROLINIANS PRIDE THEM-
SELVES ON THEIR FRIENDLINESS.
In recent years, they've had plenty
of opportunity to extend their hospitality to
newcomers, because the state's population
is rising quickly. About 50,000 people move
into South Carolina each year. They come
for the mild weather, lower housing costs, or
beautiful beaches. Many of the newcomers are
immigrants. They have arrived from nations
ranging from Mexico to Germany to Japan,
bringing an increased diversity to the state.

Where South Carolinians Live

The colors on this map indicate population density throughout the state. The darker the color, the more people live there.

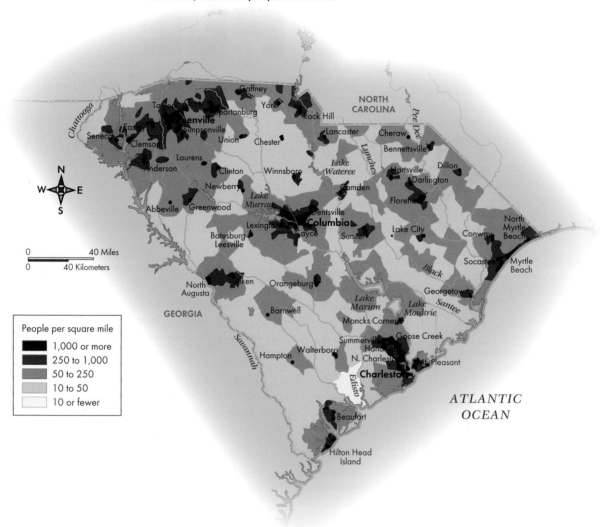

WHO LIVES IN SOUTH CAROLINA?

The majority of South Carolina's population is white (68.6 percent), with African Americans accounting for 28.7 percent of the population. The Hispanic community is growing and amounts to 3.8 percent of resi-

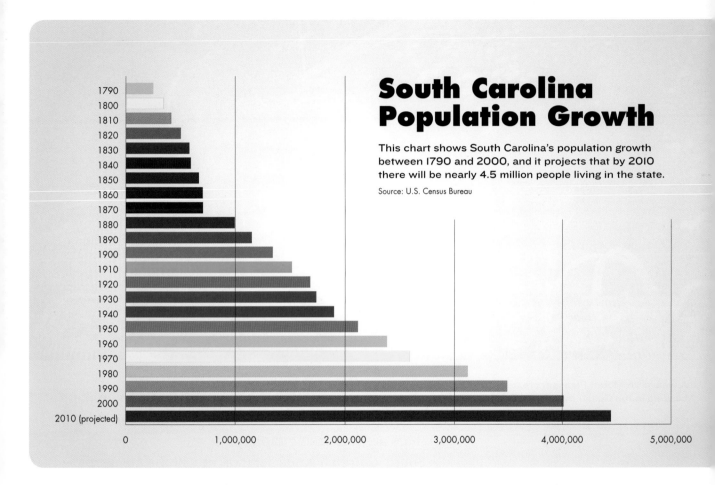

South Carolina Population Growth

This chart shows South Carolina's population growth between 1790 and 2000, and it projects that by 2010 there will be nearly 4.5 million people living in the state.

Source: U.S. Census Bureau

dents. There are also small numbers of Asians, Pacific Islanders, and Native Americans.

About two-thirds of the people in South Carolina are of European descent. Most trace their heritage to Great Britain, France, Germany, or Ireland.

In 1900, nearly six out of ten South Carolinians were African American. Many left the state in the early 20th century for better job opportunities in northern states. Today, about three out of ten South Carolinians are African American.

The majority of Hispanics in South Carolina are of Mexican ancestry. Others come from Puerto Rico,

A weaver in Mount Pleasant creates baskets in the Gullah tradition.

Big City Life

This list shows the population of South Carolina's biggest cities.

Columbia	117,088
Charleston	106,712
North Charleston	86,313
Rock Hill	59,554
Mount Pleasant	57,932

Source: U.S. Census Bureau, 2005 estimate

El Salvador, and elsewhere. Although Hispanics make up less than 4 percent of the state's population, their numbers are increasing rapidly.

South Carolina's Sea Islands are home to people whose ancestors were brought from Africa generations ago to work on South Carolina rice plantations. Known as Gullah, these people live in small farming and fishing communities along the Atlantic coast where they have preserved their African cultural heritage. They speak a language that has roots both in English and in the Krio language of Sierra Leone. They use African names and make such traditional African handicrafts as baskets and walking sticks.

About 18,000 South Carolinians are American Indian. A small number of Native American groups continue to have a presence in South Carolina. In 2005, the federal government recognized four groups

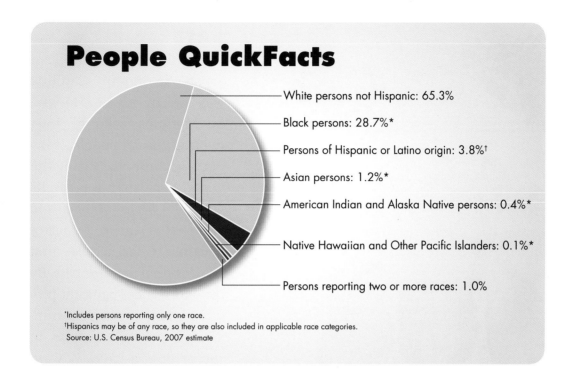

People QuickFacts

- White persons not Hispanic: 65.3%
- Black persons: 28.7%*
- Persons of Hispanic or Latino origin: 3.8%†
- Asian persons: 1.2%*
- American Indian and Alaska Native persons: 0.4%*
- Native Hawaiian and Other Pacific Islanders: 0.1%*
- Persons reporting two or more races: 1.0%

*Includes persons reporting only one race.
†Hispanics may be of any race, so they are also included in applicable race categories.
Source: U.S. Census Bureau, 2007 estimate

of South Carolina Native people as official tribes: the Eastern Cherokee, the Wassamasaw, the Waccamaw, and the Pee Dee nations. Another group, the Catawba Nation, has a reservation in York County.

EDUCATION

South Carolina has about 60 colleges and universities. The oldest college is the College of Charleston, founded in 1770. Early classes were held in Revolutionary War barracks before additional schoolrooms were built.

The University of South Carolina serves about 39,000 students on eight campuses around the state. The main campus in Columbia hosts the state's primary law school and school of medicine. Clemson, another state-supported college, has about 17,000 students. The Citadel, the state's military college, has produced many military leaders since its founding in 1842.

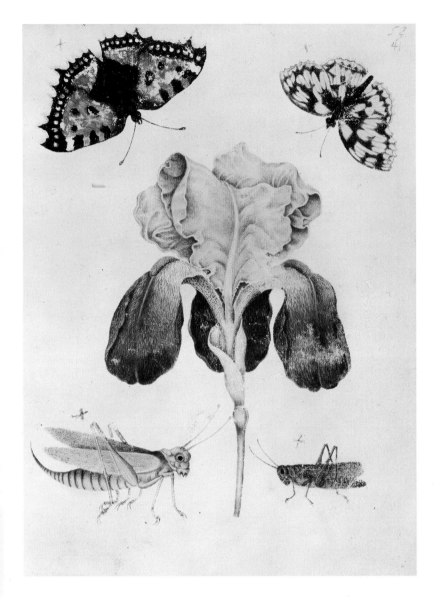

This painting by Jacques Le Moyne de Morgues, created in the mid-1500s, is from the collection at the Pierpont Morgan Library in New York City.

WORD TO KNOW

renaissance *a rebirth or renewal*

ARTS

One of the earliest European artists in South Carolina was Jacques Le Moyne de Morgues, who in 1564 painted coastal people, flowers, and animals. During the years of British rule, portraits were the art of choice, and Henrietta Deering Johnston became Charleston's first professional female artist. By the late 1700s, painters produced their artwork in miniatures, portraits that fit in the palm of a hand. Edward Malbone and Charles Fraser were known as the best of the Charleston miniature masters.

The arts flourished in Charleston during the early 20th century. Known as the Charleston **Renaissance**, this artistic movement took place between 1918 and 1941. Local artists produced landscapes, cityscapes, and etchings that attracted tourists to Charleston. Among the popular artists of the day were Alice Smith, Elizabeth Verner, and Herbert Ravenel Sass.

In 1977, Gian Carlo Menotti, Christopher Keene, and several Charlestonians founded a festival called Spoleto Festival USA. This arts festival parallels a similar event held in Spoleto, Italy. Each year, Spoleto presents a range of artistic events from visual arts to theater to dance to music.

South Carolina also has a strong folk art tradition. People have been weaving sweetgrass baskets in South Carolina for 300 years. This kind of basket making continues to be important in the Gullah culture.

MUSIC

South Carolina has a long tradition of gospel music and spirituals. Much early gospel music used shape-note singing. With this system, people needed to know only four basic notes to sing shape-note hymns. Musical notes were written as shapes—circle, square, diamond, and triangle. Singers associated the shape note with a specific tone. In the 1920s, the Dixie Hummingbirds blended old-time gospel with a new sound to create their own blues style. This style influenced the rock and roll music that would soon develop.

A crowd gathers for a performance at Spoleto Festival USA in Charleston.

James Brown (front) performs with the Famous Flames at the Apollo Theater in New York City, 1964.

MINI-BIO

DIZZY GILLESPIE: MAN WITH A HORN

John Birks "Dizzy" Gillespie (1917–1993) was born in Cheraw into a musical household. His father was a bandleader, and Gillespie began playing piano at age four and soon picked up the trumpet. A brilliant jazz musician, in the 1940s Gillespie began playing with saxophonist Charlie "Bird" Parker. Together, they explored a new musical form called bebop, which features fast notes and a lot of improvisation. Many of Gillespie's songs, such as "A Night in Tunisia" and "Salt Peanuts," are now classics.

❓ **Want to know more?** See www.pbs.org/jazz/biography/artist_id_gillespie_dizzy.htm

Bill Pinkney and the Drifters were among the many artists who founded the true South Carolina sound called beach music. Beach music is dance music, but not just any dance. In the 1950s, teens flocked to Myrtle Beach to dance a mix of the jitterbug and the Lindy that they called the shag. Today, the shag is still "the dance" at clubs along the Grand Strand.

As rock and roll became more popular, many South Carolinians could be heard on the radio and on records. Chubby Checker sang and danced "The Twist." Perhaps the greatest of South Carolina's rock artists was James Brown, known as the Godfather of Soul. Today, people also listen to tunes by Darius Rucker, once the lead singer for South Carolina's Hootie and the Blowfish.

LITERATURE

During colonial times, Charleston newspapers printed poetry, and nearly every woman who could write kept a diary or journal. The habit of keeping diaries continued through the 1800s. Many of the best sources of information about South Carolina during the Civil War are the diaries of Mary Boykin Chesnut and Floride Clemson, among others.

In the 20th century, several award-winning writers emerged in South Carolina. In 1927, DuBose Heyward won the Pulitzer Prize for his play *Porgy,* the story on which the opera *Porgy and Bess* is based. In 1929, Julia Peterkin won the Pulitzer Prize for *Scarlet Sister Mary,* a novel about the African American experience in South Carolina.

In the 1960s, James Dickey's novel *Buckdancer's Choice* won the National Book Award. Popular novelist Pat Conroy set many of his novels in South Carolina, including *Beach Music* and *The Prince of Tides.*

The state is also home to a number of children's writers. Peggy Parish created the confused but beloved housemaid Amelia Bedelia. Betsy Byars, author of the

MINI-BIO

PAT CONROY: BEST-SELLING NOVELIST

Born in Atlanta, Georgia, Pat Conroy (1945–) attended the Citadel in Charleston and then embarked on a career as a teacher in Beaufort, South Carolina. Conroy accepted a position teaching in a one-room schoolhouse on Daufuskie Island in the 1970s. He wrote about his experiences in a book called *The Water Is Wide.* Some of his other autobiographical books incorporate his experiences in South Carolina. His best-selling novel, *The Lords of Discipline,* is based on his experience at the Citadel.

 Want to know more? See www.georgiaencyclopedia.org/nge/Article.jsp?id=h-500

82

MINI-BIO

JOE FRAZIER: CHAMPION BOXER

Joe Frazier (1944–) was born near Beaufort into a sharecropping family. While working out in a gym in 1962, he was discovered by a boxing trainer. Two years later, he won a gold medal in boxing at the 1964 Summer Olympics. By 1970, Frazier was the world heavyweight champion. His greatest victory came against Muhammad Ali in a monumental bout in 1971. Frazier became a member of the International Boxing Hall of Fame in 1990.

? Want to know more? See www.ibhof.com/frazier.htm

Newbery Medal winner *The Summer of the Swans,* lives in Clemson. South Carolina native April Pulley Sayre has written more than 50 books about nature, including *Stars Beneath Your Bed: The Surprising Story of Dust* and *Dig, Wait, Listen: A Desert Toad's Tale.*

SPORTS

South Carolina does not have any major league professional sports teams, but that does not mean the state has no sports. Local high school football, soccer, basketball, and baseball draw parents and friends to the stands. On the college level,

The Clemson Tigers and University of South Carolina Gamecocks battle it out in their annual football matchup.

the state's greatest rivalry is between the Clemson Tigers and the University of South Carolina Gamecocks. Football games between these two teams generally draw crowds of 80,000 people. Smaller colleges, such as Furman, the Citadel, Wofford, and Winthrop, also have active sports teams and avid fans.

The state's golf courses are world class, as are many of the state's professional golfers. Jay Haas, Hunter Haas, and Bill Haas are a family of professional golfers from the upstate region. Dottie Pepper and Beth Daniel played for Furman University before moving on to the Ladies Professional Golf Association (LPGA). The state has 380 golf courses, ranging from professional level courses on Hilton Head and Kiawah to public courses where the average duffer can shoot for par 320 or more days a year.

The Darlington Raceway hosts NASCAR races every year. The course bears the nickname the Track Too Tough to Tame because of its rather unusual, egg-shaped racetrack. The Dodge Avenger 500, held on Mother's Day, is a major event.

South Carolina's many lakes, rivers, and coastal waters provide opportunities for sailing, waterskiing, fishing, kayaking, canoeing, and water rafting. Boating on the lakes is popular, and safety courses are offered by most schools and recreation associations.

MINI-BIO

ALTHEA GIBSON: BREAKING BARRIERS

Sumter native Althea Gibson (1927–2003) was the first African American to win tennis championships at Wimbledon, the French Open, and the U.S. Open. During her career, Gibson used her remarkable power and skill to win 11 major titles, playing both singles and doubles tennis. In 1964, she broke another barrier when she became the first African American to play in a Ladies Professional Golf Association event.

 Want to know more? See www.pbs.org/wnet/aaworld/reference/articles/althea_gibson.html

HOW TO TALK LIKE A SOUTH CAROLINIAN

Many people in South Carolina answer the telephone with "Hey!" South Carolina grandmothers are called Memaw, and many grandfathers are called Peepaw. Your "Aunt Sister" is usually your mother's sister. At the grocery store, you push your groceries in a "buggy," and when you're thirsty for a soda, no matter what variety, you ask for a "coke." In South Carolina, you also might meet "snowbirds," retirees from the North who flock to the coast each winter to enjoy the mild weather.

HOW TO EAT LIKE A SOUTH CAROLINIAN

Much of what is considered traditional South Carolina fare emerged after the Civil War. At the time, food was scarce, so many people began serving food that might have been thrown away or ignored before. People also ate grits (boiled cornmeal) and boiled turnip greens. Fatback, the fatty part of bacon, was used to season foods. South Carolinians thrived on these foods, and they have become central to South Carolinian cuisine. Other common treats include seafood, fresh produce, and boiled peanuts.

Boiled peanuts, a southern specialty, are available at stores and roadside stands.

MENU

WHAT'S ON THE MENU IN SOUTH CAROLINA?

★ ★ ★

Shrimp, oyster, and clam

Fresh seafood

Along the South Carolina coast, don't miss the fresh seafood available. Dine on shrimp, clams, oysters, and other delicious options. Calabash shrimp are small and fried, and are great with cocktail sauce.

Grits

Whenever you eat breakfast out, you'll get grits with your eggs. You make grits by boiling coarse cornmeal in water and then adding salt and a pat of butter.

Grits

Barbecue

Mustard, tomato, or vinegar? The type of barbecue sauce served depends very much on the location. In upstate South Carolina, barbecue sauce is tomato based. The midlands like a mustard base, and the coast prefers vinegar and pepper. Regardless of the sauce, Carolina barbecue is pulled or chopped pork that has been slow roasted over oak or hickory coals.

Field peas and snaps

Field peas (black-eyed or Crowder peas) and snap beans are cooked together. The liquid is called liquor. Dip corn bread in the liquor and enjoy.

Tea

Tea in South Carolina is sweet, strong, and iced. Most restaurants offer refills at no extra cost. If you want "unsweetened" tea, ask for it.

TRY THIS RECIPE
Banana Pudding

If you go to any potluck supper, mom-and-pop restaurant, or country-style establishment, you'll find banana pudding on the menu. Elsewhere in the country, the standard dessert may be apple pie, but in South Carolina, it's banana pudding. Here's a quick version you can make yourself, but be sure to have an adult nearby to help.

Ingredients:
1 package instant vanilla pudding
2 cups milk
18 vanilla wafers
1 large banana, sliced thinly into circles
1 tablespoon lemon juice

Instructions:
1. Prepare the pudding according to the directions on the box. Set it aside.
2. Line the bottom of an 8-inch-square baking dish with vanilla wafers.
3. Put the banana slices in a small plastic bag. Add the lemon juice, seal the bag, and shake. The lemon juice will keep the bananas from turning dark.
4. Cover the vanilla wafers with a layer of bananas. Pour in the pudding. Chill for 2 hours and serve.

Iced tea

READ ABOUT

Mayor Joseph Riley of Charleston (holding flag) addresses a crowd at the State House in Columbia.

CHAPTER SEVEN

GOVERNMENT

★

SOUTH CAROLINA IS A GROWING, CHANGING STATE. As more people move into the state, more schools, police and fire departments, and roads are needed. Who provides these services? The government. Newcomers to South Carolina also need jobs, and the government works to encourage new businesses to locate in the state. As the state grows, new houses are built, and some of these housing developments endanger wildlife habitat. South Carolina's government tries to balance the needs of today with a long-range vision for tomorrow.

THE CAPITOL AND THE CONSTITUTION

When Carolina was a colony, Charleston was the main city and the seat of the government. Construction of the first statehouse began in 1753. The building went into use in 1756 but burned down in 1788. By this time, a new statehouse was already being built in Columbia, the city that would be the seat of government from 1790 onward.

By the 1840s, the second statehouse was already falling apart. Work was begun on a new statehouse in 1855, but building efforts stopped as the Civil War approached. They would not be resumed until after

Capital City

This map shows places of interest in Columbia, South Carolina's capital city.

the war. The main structure was ready for use by 1875. The most stunning aspect of the capitol is the dome, a copper-covered structure at the top of the building.

South Carolina has had seven constitutions over the years. The current one dates to 1895. It has been amended, or changed, hundreds of times. The constitution divides the responsibilities of running the state into three branches: executive, legislative, and judicial.

The South Carolina State House in Columbia

THE EXECUTIVE BRANCH

The executive branch of South Carolina's government is charged with running the state government. The governor is the head of the state government. He or she is elected for a term of four years. The governor

Capitol Facts

Here are some fascinating facts about South Carolina's state capitol:

Work begun: 1855 (suspended in 1865 due to the Civil War)
Completed: 1907
Measurement: 300 feet (91 m) long, 100 feet (30 m) wide, and 180 feet (55 m) tall
Materials: Granite with a copper dome
Style: Greek Revival

South Carolina State Government

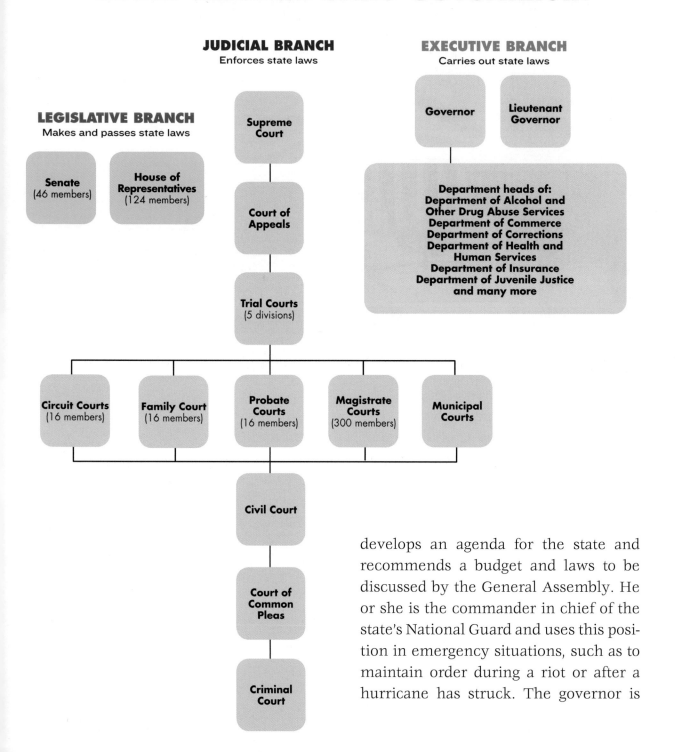

JUDICIAL BRANCH
Enforces state laws

EXECUTIVE BRANCH
Carries out state laws

LEGISLATIVE BRANCH
Makes and passes state laws

Governor

Lieutenant Governor

Senate
(46 members)

House of Representatives
(124 members)

Supreme Court

Court of Appeals

Trial Courts
(5 divisions)

Department heads of:
Department of Alcohol and Other Drug Abuse Services
Department of Commerce
Department of Corrections
Department of Health and Human Services
Department of Insurance
Department of Juvenile Justice
and many more

Circuit Courts
(16 members)

Family Court
(16 members)

Probate Courts
(16 members)

Magistrate Courts
(300 members)

Municipal Courts

Civil Court

Court of Common Pleas

Criminal Court

develops an agenda for the state and recommends a budget and laws to be discussed by the General Assembly. He or she is the commander in chief of the state's National Guard and uses this position in emergency situations, such as to maintain order during a riot or after a hurricane has struck. The governor is also spokesperson for the state, representing South Carolina interests among other states, promoting new businesses, and speaking out on public issues such as education.

South Carolinians also elect a lieutenant governor, who takes over if the governor can no longer serve. Voters also elect several other officials, including an attorney general, who is in charge of the state's legal affairs; a secretary of state, who runs elections; and a treasurer, who is in charge of the state's money. The executive branch includes many departments that deal with specific topics such as agriculture, education, and health and environmental control.

THE LEGISLATIVE BRANCH

South Carolina's legislative branch is the General Assembly, comprising the senate and the house of representatives. The senate has 46 members, and the house of representatives has 124 members. One senator is elected from each county in South Carolina, while districts for representatives are based on population.

The legislature deals with many kinds of issues. Education is a major concern. In 1999, lawmakers were worried that many children were not prepared for school when they entered kindergarten. In response, the legislature passed the South Carolina First Steps program to help preschool children prepare for the demands of school. First Steps has helped more than 410,000 students by working to improve children's health and the quality of early child care for disadvantaged children. The Countdown to Kindergarten program provides parents with a list of skills and concepts students need to succeed in school.

FAQ

Q8 HOW DID THE CAROLINA WOLF SPIDER BECOME THE OFFICIAL STATE SPIDER?

A8 In 2000, Skyler B. Hutto, a student at Sheridan Elementary School in Orangeburg, suggested that South Carolina adopt the Carolina wolf spider as its official spider. The General Assembly agreed, making South Carolina the first state to have an official spider.

Representing South Carolina

This list shows the number of elected officials who represent South Carolina, both on the state and national levels.

OFFICE	NUMBER	LENGTH OF TERM
State senators	46	4 years
State representatives	124	2 years
U.S. senators	2	6 years
U.S. representatives	6	2 years
Presidential electors	8	—

JEAN HOEFER TOAL: CHIEF JUSTICE

Jean Hoefer Toal (1943–) was born in Columbia. Early on, she showed skills that would help her as a lawyer, such as becoming the state's top debater in high school. Toal practiced law for 20 years before becoming a judge. From 1975 to 1988, she served in the South Carolina House of Representatives. She was the first woman in South Carolina to chair a standing committee of the state legislature. Then in 1988, she became the first and only woman to serve on the state supreme court. Two hears later, Toal became chief justice of the supreme court.

 Want to know more? See www.judicial.state.sc.us/supreme/displayJustice.cfm?judgeID=1118

South Carolina voters sign in so they can cast their ballots in 2008.

THE JUDICIAL BRANCH

The judicial branch of government in South Carolina consists of several levels of courts. The supreme court is the highest court in South Carolina. It has a chief justice and four associate justices who are elected to 10-year terms by the General Assembly. The terms of the justices are staggered so experienced justices are always on the court. A justice may serve any number of terms. The state supreme court reviews decisions made by lower courts, particularly in situations where the convicted person faces the death penalty. It also reviews cases concerning whether a law follows the constitution.

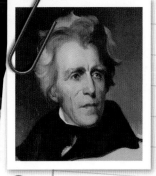

MINI-BIO

ANDREW JACKSON: SOUTH CAROLINA'S ONLY PRESIDENT

Andrew Jackson (1767–1845), the nation's seventh president, was born in the Waxhaws region. Jackson had very little formal education. As a young man, he joined the military, and he later became a hero when he led troops to defeat the British at the Battle of New Orleans during the War of 1812. He won the presidential election of 1828, becoming the first president who was not from an elite background. As president, Jackson tried to prevent wealthy businesspeople from gaining too much power. He also insisted that the federal government have power over the states. He was one of the dominant politicians of the first half of the 19th century.

 Want to know more? See www.whitehouse.gov/history/presidents/aj7.html

The court of appeals reviews cases from the circuit court and the family court. Appeals that are not heard in this court are cases that fall within the seven areas controlled by the supreme court. The court of appeals consists of a chief judge and eight associate judges who are elected by the General Assembly to staggered terms of six years each. Cases may be heard either by a panel of three judges or by all nine judges at one time.

Trial courts include circuit courts and family courts. Circuit court judges are elected by the

WACKY LAWS IN SOUTH CAROLINA

Watch out when you're in South Carolina. They have some pretty weird laws on the books! Do you think these are still enforced?

- If a man proposes marriage to a woman, by law, the marriage must take place.
- It is illegal to keep a horse in a bathtub.
- When approaching an intersection in an automated vehicle, the driver must stop 100 feet (30 m) from the intersection and fire a gun or rifle to warn horse traffic.

MINI-BIO

MARIAN WRIGHT EDELMAN: ON THE SIDE OF CHILDREN

Born in Bennettsville, Marian Wright Edelman (1939–) grew up to be a lawyer, educator, social activist, and representative for children's rights. Her father was a minister who taught her that being a Christian required service to others. In 1973, Edelman established the Children's Defense Fund (CDF) to provide disadvantaged children with a voice. The CDF researches the problems children face and proposes possible solutions. It also represents children's rights in court.

? Want to know more? See www.childrensdefense. org/site/PageNavigator/People_MWE

Representative J. Gresham Barrett speaks at a town meeting in Anderson.

General Assembly to six-year terms. Family courts hear cases concerning adoptions, divorces, child custody issues, and other similar issues. Legal cases dealing with children under the age of 17 are heard in family court.

LOCAL GOVERNMENT

Local governments provide many services to South Carolina's citizens. They run the public schools and provide police and fire protection. South

South Carolina Counties

This map shows the 46 counties in South Carolina. Columbia, the state capital, is indicated with a star.

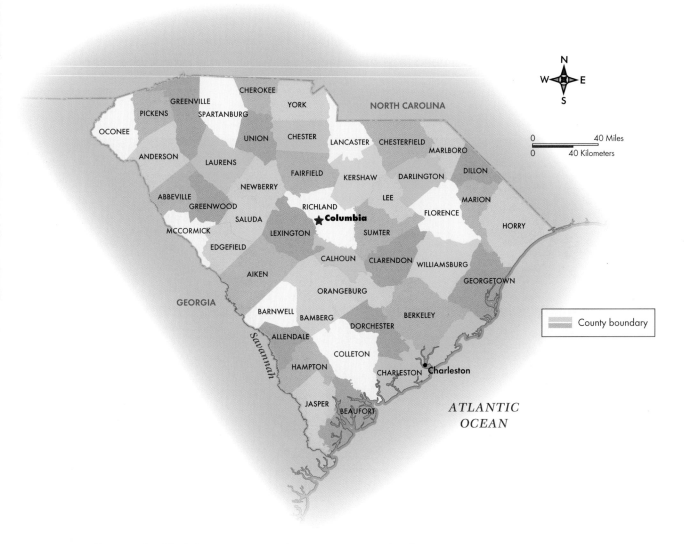

Carolina is divided into 46 counties. Most counties have an administrator or manager as well as a council or commission. Cities in South Carolina are generally run by a mayor and city council.

State Flag

The state flag shows a white palmetto tree and a white crescent on a blue background. Colonel William Moultrie developed the original design in 1775. The first flag had only the crescent. The palmetto tree was added in 1776, during the American Revolution, after American troops defended the fort made of palmetto logs on Sullivan's Island against an attack by the British navy.

TRACE IT! TRACE IT! TRACE IT!

State Seal

The state seal shows two ovals. In the left oval is a palmetto tree standing tall over a fallen tree. This scene represents the American victory over the British in the Battle of Sullivan's Island. Twelve spears representing the first 12 states in the Union are tied to the palmetto tree with a band reading *Quis Separabit?* ("Who will separate?"). The words *South Carolina* appear above this image, while below it is *Animis Opibusque Parati*, or "Ready in Soul and Resource," one of two state mottoes.

The right oval shows a woman walking along a beach where weapons are scattered about. The woman, who symbolizes hope, holds a laurel branch. Below her is the word *Spes*, or "Hope," and above is the other motto, *Dum Spiro Spero*, or "While I Breathe I Hope." Palmetto leaves connect the two ovals.

READ ABOUT

A worker in a textile mill in Columbia

CHAPTER EIGHT

ECONOMY

★

FOR MOST OF SOUTH CAROLINA'S HISTORY, ITS ECONOMY WAS BASED ON AGRICULTURE. But since the middle of the 20th century, manufacturing has taken the lead, particularly in the Greenville-Spartanburg area and around the capital. Today, South Carolinians are more likely to work in a factory making clothing, furniture, or automobile tires than they are to grow cotton. Even more South Carolinians have jobs in the service industry, working in banks, schools, restaurants, and stores.

A farmer in Lyons checks his crop of wheat.

WORD TO KNOW

gross state product *the total value of all the goods and services produced in a state*

South Carolina is the only state in the United States that grows tea.

AGRICULTURE

South Carolina has about 24,600 farms. Though farmland covers 4.8 million acres (2 million ha), it produces only 2 percent of the **gross state product**.

Among field crops, greenhouse and nursery products are the major moneymakers in South Carolina. Other major crops include tobacco, cotton, soybeans, peaches, hay, wheat, and corn. Cotton, once the king of crops in the South, is making a comeback in South Carolina. Sea Island cotton, a particularly soft strain of cotton, is prized for making clothes and linens.

Peaches, strawberries, and watermelon are some common fruits grown in the state. Farmers' markets teem with cucumbers, snap beans, collard greens, tomatoes, and melons. The state also has specialty farms producing mushrooms, gingko, and pecans.

South Carolina also produces cattle and other livestock. Roughly 415,000 head of cattle, 315,000 hogs, 213

Major Agricultural and Mining Products

This map shows where South Carolina's major agricultural and mining products come from. See a chicken? That means poultry is found there.

Urban area
Forests, some farming
Farming
Swampland, some farming

Cattle
Cotton
Dairy
Fish
Forest products
Fruit
Grains
Hogs
Manufacturing
Melons
Mineral mining
Nursery products
Oats
Poultry
Shellfish
Soybeans
Tobacco
Vegetables

million broiler chickens, and 8 million turkeys are raised in the state. Broilers are the top earners among farm animals, bringing in $563 million yearly. Dairy farms are also vital to the state's agricultural business, producing about 370 million pounds (168 million kg) of milk yearly.

SEE IT HERE!

PARK SEED

As winter rolls around, Carolinians and millions of other eager gardeners turn to the Park Seed catalog to select their flower and vegetable seeds for the following spring. But no catalog can compare with actually visiting the Park Seed Garden Center in Greenwood. Each year, gardeners swarm through rows of houseplants, seedlings, flowers, and shrubs. Park Seed is open spring, summer, and fall, and is one of the most beautiful "factories" in America!

MANUFACTURING INDUSTRY

Although agriculture is no longer the prime money-maker in South Carolina, it is closely linked to the state's manufacturing industries, providing many jobs for residents. In the state's textile mills, cotton is turned into cloth. Food products—including vegetables, meats, cheese, and milk—must be processed, packaged, distributed, and sold. Timber creates jobs in mills, pulp and paper factories, and furniture manufacturing.

For many years, the textile industry in South Carolina turned out miles of carpeting, towels, cotton cloth, sheets, and curtains. In recent years, however, the industry has faced trouble. The state has lost jobs in textile mills as more companies build mills in Mexico, Central America, and Southeast Asia. Mills in South Carolina cannot compete when they might pay their employees $9 to $15 per hour plus benefits, while mills in Mexico might pay their workers only $2 per hour with no benefits.

South Carolina has attracted manufacturers in a number of other industries, however. Cars, tires, plastic products, chemical products, **pharmaceuticals**, paper products, and machinery are all made in the state. South Carolina exports $13.5 billion of goods each year, with most products going to Canada and Mexico.

FISH AND FOREST

South Carolina has small fishing and forestry industries. Fishers bring in shrimps, crabs, oysters, and clams, as

| MINI-BIO |

ROGER MILLIKEN: TEXTILE KING

Roger Milliken (1915–) is the king of the South Carolina textile industry. Milliken inherited his family's business as a young man and built Milliken and Company into one of the largest and most successful textile corporations in the world. With an estimated personal wealth of $1 billion, he is one of the richest men in South Carolina.

 Want to know more? See www.hbs.edu/leadership/database/leaders/roger_milliken.html

Shrimp boats at Port Royal, near Beaufort

well as small numbers of eels and catfish. Much of the local seafood is sold to restaurants along the coast, but more is beginning to appear in supermarkets.

About 65 percent of the state is forested, and much of that timber is available for harvesting. Timber is the state's largest cash crop, valued at more than $876 million yearly. Softwood trees in South Carolina are turned into paper, lumber, and compressed fiberboard. Hardwoods are used to make furniture as well as to make pine tar and turpentine, which are used in some preservatives, cleaning products, and medicines.

MINING

South Carolina has no gas, oil, or natural gas reserves, nor does it have large quantities of ore, yet the state ranks 25th in the United States in total mineral value. The state is first nationally in production of cement and second in kaolin (which is used to make ceramics, paints, medicines, coated paper, and many other

WORD TO KNOW

pharmaceuticals *medicines or drugs*

The largest tires in the world—earthmover tires that measure 14 feet (4.3 m) across—are made in Lexington.

Top Products

Agriculture Greenhouse and nursery products, cotton, soybeans, tobacco, peaches, hay, wheat, and corn

Manufacturing Textiles, chemical products, pharmaceuticals, automobiles, tires

Mining Sand, gravel, clay

things). South Carolina is the only gold producer east of the Mississippi. Construction materials such as clay, gravel, sand, limestone, shale, and granite are also mined in the state. Mining occurs in 45 of the state's 46 counties.

WORD TO KNOW

radiation *particles or waves that are given off by one body and may be absorbed by another body*

SERVICES

Services are jobs that help other people. Bankers, teachers, doctors, lawyers, bus drivers, and barbers all work in service industries. Tourism is important to service industries. Hotels employ clerks, cleaning staff, and food service staff. They hire accountants and advertising agencies. Restaurants need waiters, cooks, dish-

THINK ABOUT IT!

Is Nuclear Power Safe?

South Carolina has invested in nuclear power. More than half the electricity used in the state comes from nuclear power. Much of the rest of the electricity comes from coal plants, which create pollution. Although nuclear power is cleaner, many people believe it should not be used because nuclear power plants produce dangerous waste and can release harmful **radiation** if there is an accident. They would rather see the state expand its use of solar, wind, or biofuel power. But Ann Timberlake of the Conservation Voters of South Carolina disagrees. She says:

> It's exciting that South Carolina entrepreneurs are experimenting with alternative forms of power generation: wind, solar, ocean tides, etc. But this antagonistic view of nuclear power, frankly, is irksome. None of these alternative technologies has been proven adequate to the power needs of our growing communities. And even though nuclear power generates highly toxic waste, our nation has experienced no environmental disasters from it. On-site storage of nuclear waste in high-impact cannisters has worked well. Unlike coal, nuclear power doesn't pollute air, ground or water. It may not be a perfect energy source. But it is the cleanest mass-power-generating source we have. We ought to stick with it.

What do you think South Carolina should do to meet its needs for power while maintaining a safe environment?

washers, and delivery people. Tourism attracts about 7 million visitors to the state yearly. Many people come to fish, relax on the beach, or play on one of the state's 380 golf courses. Tourism produces more than 167,000 jobs for South Carolinians.

The Port of Charleston also plays a large role in the service industry. It is the fourth-largest container port in the United States. A total of 10 million tons of cargo move through the port yearly, including oranges and grapefruit; 65,000 tons of nuts; towels; blankets; sheets; and more than 16,500 tons of candy, jams, and jellies.

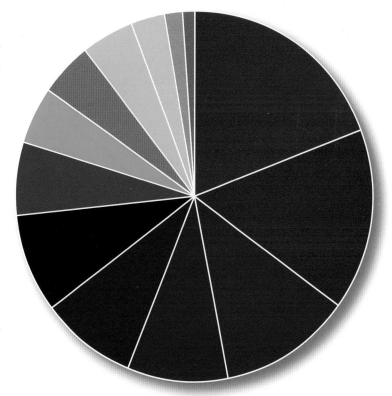

What Do South Carolinians Do?

This color-coded chart shows what industries South Carolinians work in.

19.4% Educational services, health care, and social assistance, 381,533

15.6% Manufacturing, 306,695

12.0% Retail trade, 235,945

9.1% Arts, entertainment, recreation, accommodation, and food services, 177,992

8.8% Construction, 173,229

8.6% Professional, scientific, management, administrative, and waste management services, 168,352

6.4% Finance, insurance, real estate, rental, and leasing, 125,278

4.8% Other services, except public administration, 94,554

4.7% Transportation, warehousing, and utilities, 92,854

4.7% Public administration, 92,719

3.2% Wholesale trade, 63,271

1.6% Information, 32,401

1.0% Agriculture, forestry, fishing, hunting, and mining, 19,887

Source: U.S. Census Bureau, 2006 estimate

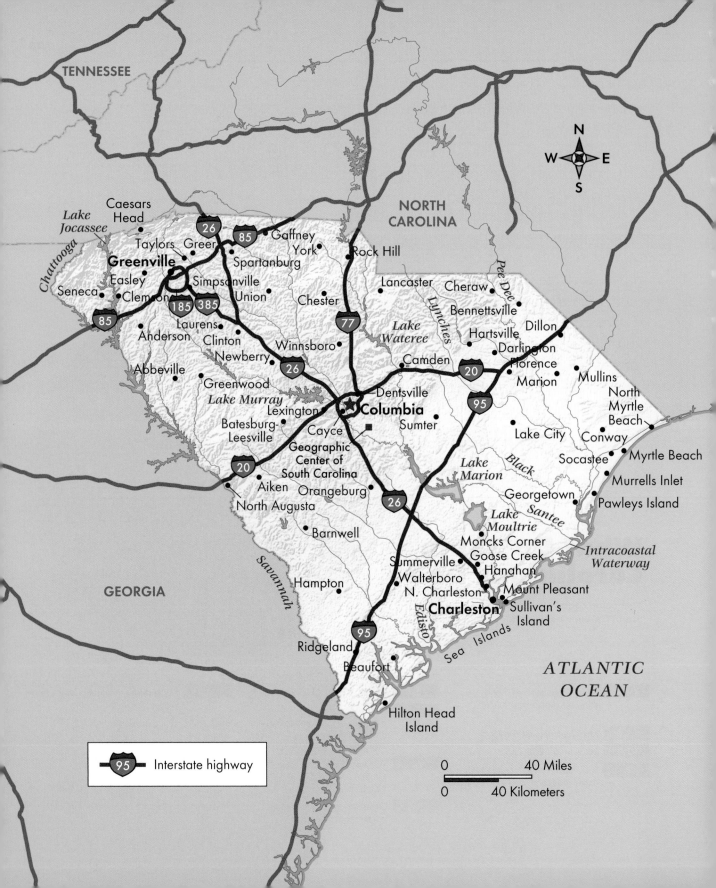

TENNESSEE

NORTH
CAROLINA

Lake Jocassee

Caesars Head

Taylors   Greer   Gaffney
York

Greenville   Spartanburg   Rock Hill

Easley   Simpsonville
Union

Seneca   Clemson

Chattooga

Lancaster   Cheraw

Bennettsville

Chester   Hartsville   Dillon

Anderson   Laurens   Darlington
Florence

Clinton   Winnsboro   *Lake Wateree*   Marion

Mullins

Newberry   Camden

North
Myrtle
Beach

Abbeville   Greenwood

Dentsville   Conway

Lake Murray   **Columbia**   Lake City   Socastee   Myrtle Beach

Lexington   Sumter   Murrells Inlet

Batesburg-
Leesville   Cayce   Pawleys Island

Geographic
Center
of
South Carolina   *Lake Marion*   Georgetown   *Black*   *Santee*   *Intracoastal Waterway*

Aiken   Orangeburg

North Augusta   *Lake Moultrie*

Barnwell   Moncks Corner

GEORGIA   Goose Creek

Hampton   Summerville   Hanahan

Walterboro   Mount Pleasant

N. Charleston   Sullivan's Island

Charleston

Savannah   *Edisto*   *Sea Islands*   **ATLANTIC OCEAN**

Ridgeland

Beaufort

Hilton Head
Island

Interstate highway

0   40 Miles

0   40 Kilometers

N
W   E
S

CHAPTER NINE

TRAVEL GUIDE

★

S OUTH CAROLINA IS KNOWN FOR ITS BEACHES, SEAFOOD, AND HOSPITALITY. From the historic streets of Charleston to the Blue Ridge Mountains, South Carolinians extend a warm welcome to one and all. Hike mountain trails, swim in the ocean, explore historic sites, or watch race cars speed around a track. From Anderson to Myrtle Beach, Hilton Head to Rock Hill, South Carolina offers year-round fun.

← Follow along with this travel map. We'll start in Charleston and travel all the way around the state to the Chattooga River.

CHARLESTON AND POINTS SOUTH

THINGS TO DO: Take a carriage ride through downtown Charleston, visit the site where the Civil War began, or see hundreds of dolphins at Hilton Head.

Charleston

★ **Magnolia Plantation:** At one of Charleston's finest plantations, you can tour the elegant home and then stroll through an herb garden, a tropical garden, a swamp garden, and a wildlife refuge.

★ **The Battery:** Take a horse-drawn carriage, rent a two-person pedal cart, or simply walk along rows of historic homes in the Battery Section of Charleston. Several of the houses, such as the Nathaniel Russell House and the Edmondston-Alston House, are

A horse and carriage on East Battery Street

open to the public. Rainbow Row, a street filled with brightly painted houses, is right around the corner.

★ **Gibbes Museum of Art:** This museum houses an outstanding collection of American art.

★ **Old City Market:** This is a lively flea market, selling everything imaginable. It is also one of the few places in the city where you can watch women perform the traditional art of weaving sweetgrass into baskets.

★ **Charles Towne Landing:** This park stands on the original site of Charleston. You can take a guided tour of the original fortress from 1670, as well as miles of gardens, an animal forest (featuring animals from colonial days), and a replica of a 17th-century trading vessel.

★ **Fort Sumter:** Hop on a ferry to reach the fort where the Civil War began. Fort Sumter National Monument is a tribute to the Civil War and all the people who fought in it.

★ **South Carolina Aquarium:** Here you'll find 10,000 animals and 5,000 plants all in a stunning setting. This aquarium features 60 exhibits that focus on the state's swamps, rivers, lakes, and shore.

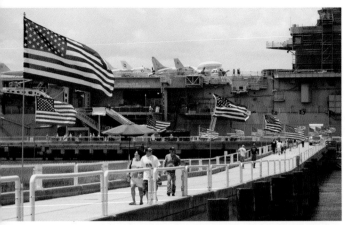

The USS *Yorktown*

Sullivan's Island

★ **Patriots Point:** The USS *Yorktown*, an aircraft carrier that served during World War II, lies at anchor at Patriots Point. Exploring the ship and the Maritime Museum, you will learn about the sea and the history of sea travel.

Hilton Head Island

★ **Dolphin Head:** Hundreds, perhaps thousands, of dolphins sometimes swim in the waters of Port Royal Sound. Dolphin Head, a craggy highland, overlooks the sound.

Sea Islands

★ **Penn Center Historic District:** Located on St. Helena Island, Penn Center is a national historic district and a center of the Gullah culture. This site is a living museum, where the language, culture, and history of the island's African American population are preserved.

★ **Daufuskie Island:** Hop aboard the *Adventure* and take a tour of the island. You will experience the Sea Islands as they were first seen by arriving settlers.

THE GRAND STRAND

THINGS TO DO: Play golf, go to a rice museum, or see alligators up close.

Myrtle Beach

★ **Golf courses:** Some of the most beautiful, challenging, and frustrating courses in the state are found in the Myrtle Beach area. But don't try to get a ball out of a water trap—that floating log is most likely an alligator.

The golf course at Island Green Country Club

★ **Alligator Adventure:** Reptile lovers, this is the place for you. There are alligators of every size imaginable, including some massive creatures that measure 20 feet (6 m) long. Snakes, turtles, and lizards also reside here.

★ **Broadway at the Beach:** This outdoor center offers dining, shopping, and boat rentals. You'll find theme rides reminiscent of the Myrtle Beach Pavilion that closed in 2006. Also there is Ripley's Aquarium, which features a walk-through tunnel where fish swim all around you.

Murrells Inlet

★ **Brookgreen Gardens:** At this vast park, you'll find formal gardens featuring more than 2,000 species of plants and 800 sculptures, as well as a wildlife center.

Brookgreen Gardens

Huntington Beach State Park

★ **Huntington Beach State Park:** Enjoy a day at this beautiful beach that offers swimming, camping, and bird-watching. You'll also find Atalaya, home of philanthropist Archer Huntington and artist Anna Hyatt Huntington, and an environmental education center.

Pawleys Island

★ **The shops:** Pawleys Island is a place for rocking slowly in a hammock, walking on the beach, and eating great seafood. When you get bored, head to the shops that sell clothing made of Sea Island cotton, hammocks, and local crafts.

Georgetown

★ **Rice Museum:** At this museum, you can learn all about how rice is planted and harvested.

★ **Hampton Plantation:** Now a state park, the Hampton Plantation was originally built in 1700. At this park, you can learn about South Carolina's colonial rice-growing industry and the lives of the enslaved Africans who made it profitable.

THE MIDLANDS

THINGS TO DO: Canoe through a swamp, learn about African American culture, or eat some world-class barbecue.

SEE IT HERE!

RIVERBANKS ZOO AND GARDEN

At this zoo, animals live in enclosures that reflect their native habitats. Giraffes, zebras, and ostriches roam plains. Koalas and wallabies share their homes with other native Australian animals. Walk through the lorikeet **aviary** and discover some of Australia's most beautiful birds. At the botanical garden, you can relax in the peaceful Shade Garden, enjoy the beauty of the Walled Garden, and get a feel for desert life in the Dry Garden.

WORD TO KNOW

aviary *a large walk-in enclosure where birds have room to fly*

Congaree Swamp National Monument

Columbia

★ **Congaree Swamp National Monument:** Congaree Swamp is the largest old-growth floodplain forest in the United States. Walk or canoe among the ancient giant cypress trees.

★ **Maurice's Gourmet Piggie Park Barbecue:** This restaurant has been named one of the top barbecue places in the United States. Go hungry—you'll get plenty of true South Carolina pulled or chopped pork barbecue, coleslaw, fries, sweet tea, and a bun.

★ **Columbia Museum of Art:** This museum features art from the United States and around the world. Highlights include many Italian paintings from the 15th and 16th centuries.

South Carolina State Museum

★ **South Carolina State Museum:**
This museum houses art, natural
history, cultural history, and science and technology. The Stringer
Discovery Center is hands-on and
lots of fun.

★ **Mann-Simons Cottage:** In the
heart of downtown Columbia, the
Mann-Simons Cottage is a pre–Civil
War house that was owned by free
African Americans in the city.
Today, it is an African American
heritage center.

Sumter

★ **Swan Lake Iris Gardens:** In the
spring, do not miss this stunning
garden. Seven species of swans
glide on the garden ponds amid 25
species of irises.

Cheraw

★ **Sand Hills State Forest:** This
forest and wildlife refuge is the
home of the endangered red-
cockaded woodpecker. The forest
also provides homes for dozens of
kinds of reptiles and amphibians.
Twenty-five species of nonvenom-
ous snakes live in the Sand Hills,
along with venomous copperheads,
cottonmouths, and rattlesnakes.
Bird-watchers visit the forest to
look for the 190 species that have
been spotted in this refuge.

Florence

★ **Pee Dee State Farmers' Market:**
Farmers from throughout the region
bring their fresh vegetables, jams,
and jellies to the Pee Dee market.
This is a place to buy southern deli-
cacies such as collard greens, boiled
peanuts, and fresh okra.

Petunias for sale at the Pee Dee State Farmers' Market

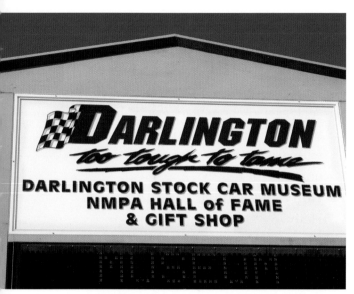

Darlington Stock Car Museum NMPA Hall of Fame

Darlington

★ **Stock Car Museum NMPA Hall of Fame:** This is a must-see for racing fans. Visitors can find the National Motorsports Press Association Hall of Fame, with photos, memorabilia, and interactive exhibits showcasing NASCAR racing and its greatest drivers.

Camden

★ **Historic Camden:** During the American Revolution, Camden was a center of activity. Today, the old fort and village are part of the Historic Camden Revolutionary War Site.

Q: WHAT ARE THE MICE ON MAIN?

A: Downtown Greenville has nine mice made out of bronze hidden in plain sight. This idea was a school project done by Christ Church Episcopal School senior Jimmy Ryan. He suggested placing the mice downtown for children to hunt. He raised the money and hired local sculptor Zan Wells to make the bronze mice. Here's a hint: You'll find one on the fountain in front of a downtown hotel.

THE UPSTATE

THINGS TO DO: Hunt for bronze mice, see a musical, or visit a colonial plantation.

Greenville

★ **The Pavilion:** Here you can ice-skate, play tennis, and ride the Brushy Creek & Southern miniature railroad.

★ **Roper Mountain Science Center:** Run by the Greenville County School District, the science center offers hands-on and attention-grabbing science programs to school-age children. The planetarium has a show every Friday night.

★ **Peace Center:** Concerts, dance, and theater are offered at this state-of-the-art theater complex. The Peace Center has a children's theater, and it is the home of the Greenville Symphony Orchestra.

★ **Shoeless Joe Jackson Memorial Park:** This park pays homage to Chicago White Sox great "Shoeless Joe" Jackson, who grew up in a textile mill community and played on the Brandon Mill baseball team.

Spartanburg

★ **Walnut Grove Plantation:** During a tour of this 18th-century plantation, you can visit outbuildings such as a kitchen, blacksmith shop, wheat house, barn, springhouse with dry cellar, school, and doctor's quarters.

★ **Hollywild Animal Park:** Hollywild's many animals appear in television shows and films. Lions, elephants, giraffes, hyenas, and many other creatures live at the park.

★ **Hatcher Garden and Woodland Preserve:** Ten thousand plants decorate an array of hiking trails in Hatcher Garden. Many people come to enjoy the refreshing waterfall.

Hatcher Garden and Woodland Preserve

MINI-BIO

"SHOELESS JOE" JACKSON: TRIUMPH AND DISGRACE

"Shoeless Joe" Jackson (1888–1951) was born in Pickens County and became one of the greatest baseball players of his time. He and seven other members of the Chicago White Sox were accused of taking bribes to intentionally lose the 1919 World Series. Jackson claimed he knew about the scheme but refused to take part. He and the players who had been involved were banned from baseball for life. Jackson's career batting average was .356, and he would have been a shoo-in for the Baseball Hall of Fame had it not been for the "Black Sox" scandal.

Want to know more? See www.chicagohs.org/history/blacksox/joe.html

A Place For All Seasons

Anderson

★ **Lake Hartwell:** This lake is ideal for boating, sailing, fishing, water-skiing, and picnics.

Abbeville

★ **The Abbeville Opera House:** At the beginning of the 20th century, this opera house attracted acts from major cities throughout the United States. Today, it is home to a theater group, and features musicals and comedies throughout the year.

THE BLUE RIDGE

THINGS TO DO: Go white-water rafting, hike up a mountain, or go on a picnic.

Caesars Head

★ **Caesars Head State Park:** Autumn is the time for Caesars Head. A huge rock outcrop overlooks the dramatic, colorful landscape. Autumn is also the time for the annual Hawk Watch. Visitors will never forget watching soaring, swirling hawks, kites, falcons, and eagles on their migration.

The Chattooga River

★ **White-water rafting:** River rafting on the Chattooga River is like a wet, wild roller-coaster ride. In the spring, rides are quick paced and exhilarating, as the river rushes with snowmelt. Summer and fall are milder but equally entertaining.

The Lakes

★ **Lake Jocassee:** Here you can rent a boat or go fishing for trout and smallmouth bass. The water is crystal clear, deep, and usually pretty cold. The area also has a number of hiking trails with lovely waterfalls.

★ **Keowee-Toxaway State Park:** This park features two large lakes where camping, hiking, fishing, and water sports are popular. A museum tells the story of the Cherokee people and their heritage.

The view of Lake Jocassee from Devils Fork State Park

WRITING PROJECTS

Check out these ideas for creating a campaign brochure and writing you-are-there narratives. Or research the lives of famous South Carolinians.

118

ART PROJECTS

You can illustrate the state song, create a dazzling PowerPoint presentation, or learn about the state quarter and design your own.

119

TIMELINE

What happened when? This timeline highlights important events in the state's history—and shows what was happening throughout the United States at the same time.

122

GLOSSARY

Remember the Words to Know from the chapters in this book? They're all collected here.

125

FAST FACTS

Use this section to find fascinating facts about state symbols, land area and population statistics, weather, sports teams, and much more.

126

SCIENCE, TECHNOLOGY, & MATH PROJECTS

Make weather maps, graph population statistics, and research endangered species that live in the state.

120

PRIMARY VS. SECONDARY SOURCES

121

So what are primary and secondary sources? And what's the diff? This section explains all that and where you can find them.

BIOGRAPHICAL DICTIONARY

133

This at-a-glance guide highlights some of the state's most important and influential people. Visit this section and read about their contributions to the state, the country, and the world.

RESOURCES

Books, Web sites, DVDs, and more. Take a look at these additional sources for information about the state.

137

WRITING PROJECTS

★ ★ ★

Write a Memoir, Journal, or Editorial for Your School Newspaper!

Picture Yourself . . .

★ Preparing for a Green Corn Festival. Describe all the hard work that led up to this celebration. Also describe what takes place at the ceremony.

  SEE: Chapter Two, pages 29–30.

  GO TO: http://nativeamericans.mrdonn.org/greencorn.html

★ As Harvey Gantt, the first African American student to attend Clemson University, or as Shannon Faulkner, the first woman admitted to the Citadel. Describe some of the greatest challenges you'd face. What motivates you to continue the struggle?

  SEE: Chapter Five, pages 68–69, 70.

  GO TO: www.scafricanamericanhistory.com/currenthonoree.asp?month=2&year=1994 and www.now.org/nnt/08-95/citadel.html

Create an Election Brochure or Web Site!

Run for office! Throughout this book, you've read about some of the issues that concern South Carolina today. As a candidate for governor of South Carolina, create a campaign brochure or Web site.

★ Explain how you meet the qualifications to be governor of South Carolina.

★ Talk about the three or four major issues you'll focus on if you're elected.

★ Remember, you'll be responsible for South Carolina's budget. How would you spend the taxpayers' money?

  SEE: Chapter Seven, pages 89–91.

  GO TO: South Carolina's government Web site at www.sc.gov. You might also want to read some local newspapers. Try these:

  The Post and Courier at www.charleston.net

  The State at www.thestate.com

Create an interview script with a famous person from South Carolina!

★ Research various influential South Carolinians, such as Attakullakulla, Eliza Lucas Pinckney, Mary McLeod Bethune, Septima Poinsette Clark, James Brown, Joe Frazier, Althea Gibson, Roger Milliken, "Shoeless Joe" Jackson, and many others.

★ Based on your research, pick one person you would most like to talk with.

★ Write a script of the interview. What questions would you ask? How would this person answer? Create a question-and-answer format. You may want to supplement this writing project with a voice-recording dramatization of the interview.

  SEE: Chapters Three, Five, Six, Eight, Nine, pages 40, 43, 66, 70, 80–81, 82, 83, 102, 114, and the Biographical Dictionary, pages133–136.

  GO TO: www.sciway.net/hist

ART PROJECTS

★ ★ ★

Create a PowerPoint Presentation or Visitors' Guide

Welcome to South Carolina!

South Carolina's a great place to visit and to live! From its natural beauty to its historic sites, there's plenty to see and do. In your PowerPoint presentation or brochure, highlight 10 to 15 of South Carolina's fascinating landmarks. Be sure to include:

★ a map of the state showing where these sites are located

★ photos, illustrations, Web links, natural history facts, geographic stats, climate and weather, plants and wildlife, and recent discoveries

SEE: Chapter Nine, pages 106–115, and Fast Facts, pages 126–127.

GO TO: The official tourism Web site for South Carolina at www.discoversouthcarolina.com. Download and print maps, photos, and vacation ideas for tourists.

Illustrate the Lyrics to the South Carolina State Songs

("Carolina" and "South Carolina on My Mind")

Use markers, paints, photos, collages, colored pencils, or computer graphics to illustrate the lyrics to one of the state songs. Turn your illustrations into a picture book, or scan them into PowerPoint and add music.

SEE: The lyrics to "Carolina" and "South Carolina on My Mind" on page 128.

GO TO: The Web site at www.sc.gov to find out more about the origins of the state songs.

State Quarter Project

From 1999 to 2008, the U.S. Mint introduced new quarters commemorating each of the 50 states in the order that they were admitted to the Union. Each state's quarter features a unique design on its back, or reverse.

GO TO: www.usmint.gov/kids and find out what's featured on the back of the South Carolina quarter.

★ Research the significance of the image. Who designed the quarter? Who chose the final design?

★ Design your own South Carolina quarter. What images would you choose for the reverse?

★ Make a poster showing the South Carolina quarter and label each image.

SCIENCE, TECHNOLOGY, & MATH PROJECTS

★ ★ ★

Graph Population Statistics!

★ Compare population statistics (such as ethnic background, birth, death, and literacy rates) in South Carolina counties or major cities.

★ In your graph or chart, look at population density and write sentences describing what the population statistics show; graph one set of population statistics and write a paragraph explaining what the graphs reveal.

SEE: Chapter Six, pages 74–77.

GO TO: The official Web site for the U.S. Census Bureau at www.census.gov and at http://quickfacts.census.gov/qfd/states/45000.html to find out more about population statistics, how they work, and what the statistics are for South Carolina.

Create a Weather Map of South Carolina!

Use your knowledge of South Carolina's geography to research and identify conditions that result in specific weather events. What is it about the geography of South Carolina that makes it vulnerable to hurricanes? Create a weather map or poster that shows the weather patterns over the state. Include a caption explaining the technology used to measure weather phenomena and provide data.

SEE: Chapter One, pages 16–17.

GO TO: The National Oceanic and Atmospheric Administration's National Weather Service Web site at www.weather.gov for weather maps and forecasts for South Carolina.

Track Endangered Species

Using your knowledge of South Carolina's wildlife, research which animals and plants are endangered or threatened.

★ Find out what the state is doing to protect these species.

★ Chart known populations of the animals and plants, and report on changes in certain geographic areas.

SEE: Chapter One, page 18.

GO TO: Web sites such as http://ecos.fws.gov/tess_public/StateListingAndOccurrence.do?state=SC for lists of endangered species in South Carolina.

Piping plover

PRIMARY VS. SECONDARY SOURCES

★ ★ ★

What's the Diff?

Your teacher may require at least one or two primary sources and one or two secondary sources for your assignment. So, what's the difference between the two?

★ **Primary sources are original.** You are reading the actual words of someone's diary, journal, letter, autobiography, or interview. Primary sources can also be photographs, maps, prints, cartoons, news/film footage, posters, first-person newspaper articles, drawings, musical scores, and recordings. By the way, when you conduct a survey, interview someone, shoot a video, or take photographs to include in a project, you are creating primary sources!

★ **Secondary sources are what you find in encyclopedias, textbooks, articles, biographies, and almanacs.** These are written by a person or group of people who tell about something that happened to someone else. Secondary sources also recount what another person said or did. This book is an example of a secondary source.

Now that you know what primary sources are—where can you find them?

★ **Your school or local library:** Check the library catalog for collections of original writings, government documents, musical scores, and so on. Some of this material may be stored on microfilm. The Library of Congress Web site (www.loc.gov) is an excellent online resource for primary source materials.

★ **Historical societies:** These organizations keep historical documents, photographs, and other materials. Staff members can help you find what you are looking for. History museums are also great places to see primary sources firsthand.

★ **The Internet:** There are lots of sites that have primary sources you can download and use in a project or assignment.

TIMELINE

★ ★ ★

U.S. Events

South Carolina Events

11,000 BCE

Mississippian gorget

c. 11,000 BCE
Humans arrive in what is now South Carolina.

8000 BCE

c. 8000 BCE
The Archaic culture develops.

2000 BCE

c. 2000 BCE
Native people build the Spanish Mount, a large mound made of shells.

1000 BCE

c. 1000 BCE
The Woodland culture develops.

1 CE

c. 900 CE
The Mississippian culture develops.

1400

1400s
Between 15,000 and 20,000 Native people live in what is now South Carolina.

1492

Christopher Columbus and his crew sight land in the Caribbean Sea.

1500

1521
Spanish explorers become the first Europeans to land in what is now South Carolina.

1540
Spaniard Hernando de Soto leads an expedition into South Carolina.

Hernando de Soto

1562
French Huguenots build Charlesfort on what is now Parris Island.

1565

Spanish admiral Pedro Menéndez de Avilés founds St. Augustine, Florida, the oldest continuously occupied European settlement in the continental United States.

1600

1663
The Lords Proprietors get a charter from King Charles II to found Carolina Colony.

U.S. Events

South Carolina Events

1670
The English begin settling Carolina.

1682
René-Robert Cavelier, Sieur de La Salle, claims more than 1 million square miles (2.6 million sq km) of territory in the Mississippi River basin for France, naming it Louisiana.

1685
Rice is first brought to Carolina.

1700

1715
The Yamassee War begins.

1739
Enslaved Africans take part in a revolt called the Stono Rebellion.

1776
Thirteen American colonies declare their independence from Great Britain.

1776
Colonists win the Battle of Sullivan's Island, their first victory in the American Revolution.

1787
The U.S. Constitution is written.

1788
South Carolina becomes the eighth state in the Union.

1800

1803
The Louisiana Purchase almost doubles the size of the United States.

early 1800s
Cotton becomes South Carolina's major crop.

1860
South Carolina is the first state to secede.

1861-65
The American Civil War is fought between the Northern Union and the Southern Confederacy; it ends with the surrender of the Confederate army, led by General Robert E. Lee.

1861
The Civil War begins at Fort Sumter.

1868
Francis Cardozo is the first African American to hold statewide office in the United States.

1886
Apache leader Geronimo surrenders to the U.S. Army, ending the last major Native American rebellion against the expansion of the United States into the West.

1895
South Carolina writes a new constitution that allows segregation.

U.S. Events `1900` South Carolina Events

U.S. Events

1917–18
The United States engages in World War I.

1929
The stock market crashes, plunging the United States more deeply into the Great Depression.

1941–45
The United States engages in World War II.

1951–53
The United States engages in the Korean War.

1954
The U.S. Supreme Court prohibits segregation of public schools in the *Brown v. Board of Education* ruling.

1964–73
The United States engages in the Vietnam War.

1991
The United States and other nations engage in the brief Persian Gulf War against Iraq.

`2000`

2001
Terrorists hijack four U.S. aircraft and crash them into the World Trade Center in New York City, the Pentagon in Arlington, Virginia, and a Pennsylvania field, killing thousands.

2003
The United States and coalition forces invade Iraq.

South Carolina Events

1910–40
About 250,000 African Americans leave South Carolina during the Great Migration.

1920s
A boll weevil infestation devastates the state's cotton industry.

Cotton bolls

1963
Harvey Gantt becomes the first African American admitted to Clemson University.

1989
Hurricane Hugo hits South Carolina.

1995
The U.S. Supreme Court forces the Citadel to admit women.

1999
Civil rights groups begin a boycott to attempt to force South Carolina to stop flying the Confederate flag.

2000–07
South Carolina loses 5,000 textile jobs.

Confederate flag

GLOSSARY

aviary a large walk-in enclosure where birds have room to fly

boycott the organized refusal to use a service or buy a product, as a form of protest

breechcloths garments worn by men over their lower bodies

civil rights basic human rights that all citizens in a society are entitled to, such as the right to vote

desegregate to end the practice of keeping races separate from each other in education or other community activities

endangered describing a species in danger of becoming extinct

entrepreneur someone who manages and takes the risk of starting a business

fasted went without eating

gross state product the total value of all the goods and services produced in a state

guerrilla describing soldiers who don't belong to regular armies; they often use surprise attacks and other uncommon battle tactics

hardtack dried biscuits

indentured servants people who work for others under contract

larvae newly hatched young of an animal that look very different from the adult

nutrients substances that nourish a plant or animal

pharmaceuticals medicines or drugs

plateau an elevated part of the earth with steep slopes

precipitation all water that falls to the earth, including rain, sleet, hail, snow, dew, fog, or mist

radiation particles or waves that are given off by one body and may be absorbed by another body

rationed controlled the amount one could use

renaissance a rebirth or renewal

sediments material eroded from rocks and deposited elsewhere by wind, water, or glaciers

segregation separation from others, according to race, class, ethnic group, religion, or other factors

strike an organized refusal to work, usually as a sign of protest about working conditions

textile cloth or fabric that is woven, knitted, or otherwise manufactured

threatened describing a species that is likely to become endangered in the foreseeable future

tributaries smaller rivers that flow into a larger river

FAST FACTS

★ ★ ★

State Symbols

State seal

Statehood date	May 23, 1788, the 8th state
Origin of state name	From *Carolanus*, Latin for "Charles"; named to honor Charles I of England
State capital	Columbia
State nickname	Palmetto State
State mottoes	*Animis Opibusque Parati* (Ready in Soul and Resource); *Dum Spiro Spero* (While I Breathe I Hope)
State bird	Carolina wren
State flower	Carolina (yellow) jessamine
State animal	White-tailed deer
State gem	Amethyst
State stone	Blue granite
State fish	Striped bass
State songs	"Carolina" and "South Carolina on My Mind"
State tree	Palmetto
State fair	Mid-October at Columbia

Geography

Total area; rank	32,020 square miles (82,931 sq km); 40th
Land; rank	30,110 square miles (77,985 sq km); 40th
Water; rank	1,911 square miles (4,949 sq km); 21st
Inland water; rank	1,008 square miles (2,611 sq km); 21st
Coastal water; rank	72 square miles (186 sq km); 18th
Territorial water; rank	831 square miles (2,152 sq km); 11th
Geographic center	Richland, 13 miles (21 km) southeast of Columbia
Latitude	32°5' N to 35°25' N
Longitude	78°40' W to 83°30' W
Highest point	Sassafras Mountain, 3,560 feet (1,085 m) located in Pickens County
Lowest point	Sea level along the Atlantic Ocean

Largest city Columbia
Number of counties 46
Longest river Savannah River, 238 miles (383 km)

Population

Population; rank (2007 estimate) 4,407,709; 24th
Density (2007 estimate) 146 persons per square mile (56 per sq km)
Population distribution (2000 census) 60% urban, 40% rural
Race (2007 estimate) White persons: 68.6%*
Black persons: 28.7%*
Asian persons: 1.2%*
American Indian and Alaska Native persons: 0.4%*
Native Hawaiian and Other Pacific Islanders: 0.1%*
Persons reporting two or more races: 1.0%
Persons of Hispanic or Latino origin: 3.8%†
White persons not Hispanic: 65.3%

Includes persons reporting only one race.
† Hispanics may be of any race, so they are also included in applicable race categories.

Weather

Record high temperature 111°F (44°C) in Blackville on September 4, 1925; at Calhoun Falls on September 8, 1925; and at Camden on June 28, 1954
Record low temperature −19°F (−28°C) at Caesars Head on January 21, 1985
Average July temperature 82°F (28°C)
Average January temperature 48°F (9°C)
Average yearly precipitation 51 inches (130 cm)

State flag

STATE SONG

★ ★ ★

South Carolina has two state songs. "Carolina," with words by Henry Timrod and music by Anne Custis Burgess, was adopted in 1911. "South Carolina on My Mind," written by Hank Martin and Buzz Arledge, was adopted in 1984.

"Carolina"

The despot treads thy sacred sands,
Thy pines give shelter to his bands;
Thy sons stand by with idle hands,
Carolina!
He breathes at ease thy airs of balm,
He scorns the lances of thy palm;
Oh! who shall break thy craven calm,
Carolina!
Thy ancient fame is growing dim,
A spot is on thy garment's rim;
Give to the winds thy battle-hymn,
Carolina!

"South Carolina on My Mind"

At the foot hills of the Appalachian chain,
Down through the rivers, to the coastal plain,
There's a place that I call home,
And I'll never be alone,
Singin' this Carolina love song

I've got South Carolina on my mind
Remembering all those sunshine
   Summertimes,
And the Autumns in the Smokies when the
   leaves turn to gold
Touches my heart and thrills my soul to have
   South Carolina on my mind,
With those clean snow-covered mountain
   Wintertimes
And the white sand of the beaches and those
   Carolina peaches,
I've got South Carolina on my mind.

NATURAL AREAS AND HISTORIC SITES

★ ★ ★

National Park

Congaree National Park is the largest remnant of old-growth floodplain forest remaining on the continent. The trees tower to record size amid astonishing natural beauty.

National Monuments

Fort Sumter National Monument commemorates the site of the first engagement in the American Civil War in 1861.

Fort Moultrie National Monument preserves the site of the first American victory during the Revolution. The monument provides visitors with an opportunity to learn how coastal defenses have evolved at this site.

National Battlefield

Cowpens National Battlefield is the site of a decisive American victory in the Revolutionary War.

National Military Park

Kings Mountain National Military Park is the site of a colonial victory in 1780 during the Revolutionary War.

National Historic Sites

Charles Pinckney National Historic Site preserves the home of one of the main authors of the U.S. Constitution.

Ninety Six National Historic Site is the site of an early frontier trading post and two battles during the Revolutionary War.

National Historic Trail

The *Overmountain Victory National Historic Trail* follows the route American soldiers took from Virginia to the Battle of Kings Mountain in South Carolina during the Revolutionary War.

National Forests

South Carolina has two national forests within its borders: *Sumter National Forest* and *Francis Marion National Forest*, which is named for the Revolutionary War general.

State Parks

South Carolina's state park system features and maintains 46 state parks and recreation areas, including *Table Rock State Park*, a scenic area of mountains and dense forests; *General Thomas Sumter Memorial Park*, which includes the gravesite of the Revolutionary War leader; and *Andrew Jackson State Park*, which is in the region where the U.S. president was born.

SPORTS TEAMS

★ ★ ★

NCAA Teams (Division I)

Charleston Southern University *Buccaneers*
The Citadel *Bulldogs*
Clemson *Tigers*
Coastal Carolina *Chanticleers*
College of Charleston *Cougars*
Furman University *Paladins*
South Carolina State University *Bulldogs*
University of South Carolina *Gamecocks*
Winthrop *Eagles*
Wofford College *Terriers*

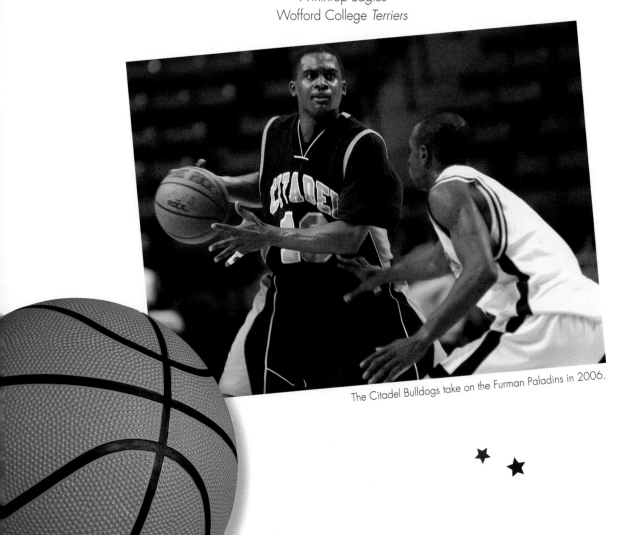

The Citadel Bulldogs take on the Furman Paladins in 2006.

CULTURAL INSTITUTIONS

Libraries

The *Charleston Library Society*, one of the first municipal libraries in America, was founded in 1748 and is still in operation.

The *South Carolina State Library* (Columbia) has a large South Carolina collection and a government publications section, as well as a general collection.

Museums

The *Charleston Museum* houses a collection of South Carolina memorabilia.

The *Gibbes Museum of Art* (Charleston) focuses primarily on American art from the South.

The *Mann-Simons Cottage* (Columbia) is a museum of African American culture, emphasizing the life of free blacks in South Carolina.

The *South Carolina State Museum* (Columbia) contains works by South Carolina artists along with exhibits on science and industry.

Performing Arts

South Carolina has one major symphony orchestra and one major opera company.

Universities and Colleges

In 2006, South Carolina had 33 public and 27 private institutions of higher learning.

ANNUAL EVENTS

January–March

Lowcountry Oyster Festival in Charleston (late January)

Garden Tours, statewide (February–May)

Canadian-American Days Festival at Myrtle Beach (March)

Dodge Dealers 400 stock car race in Darlington (late March)

Plantation Tours, statewide (March–April)

April–June

Polo Games in Aiken (April to June)

The Governor's Annual Frog Jumping Contest in Springfield (Saturday before Easter)

Blessing of the Fleet and Seafood Festival in Mount Pleasant (late April)

Iris Festival in Sumter (May)

Gullah Cultural Festival in Beaufort (late May)

Spoleto Festival USA in Charleston (May–June)

Sun Fun Festival in Myrtle Beach (June–September)

July–September

Peach Festival in Gaffney (early July)

Little Mountain Reunion in Little Mountain (first Saturday in August)

Scottish Games and Highland Gathering at Middleton Place Gardens near Charleston (mid-September)

October–December

State Fair in Columbia (mid-October)

Colonial Cup in Camden (November)

Chitlin' Strut in Salley (Saturday after Thanksgiving)

Spoleto Festival USA

BIOGRAPHICAL DICTIONARY

Attakullakulla (c.1700–c. 1780) was a Cherokee leader who helped his people negotiate with white settlers.

Bernard Baruch (1870–1965), a native of Camden, became wealthy working in the financial industry. He was also a close adviser of Presidents Woodrow Wilson and Franklin D. Roosevelt.

Mary McLeod Bethune See page 66.

Blackbeard See page 39.

Charles F. Bolden Jr. (1946–) is an astronaut who took part in four space flights, logging more than 680 hours in space. He is from Columbia.

James Brown (1933–2006) was born in Barnwell and is remembered as one of the most influential musicians of the 20th century. He was known as the King of Funk and the Godfather of Soul. Some of his best-known songs are "Papa's Got a Brand New Bag" and "I Got You (I Feel Good)."

Charles Bolden Jr.

James F. Byrnes (1879–1972) was a statesman who served as U.S. senator, governor of South Carolina, a U.S. Supreme Court justice, and secretary of state in the Harry Truman administration. He was born in Charleston.

John C. Calhoun (1782–1850), who was born near Abbeville, was one of the leading politicians of his time. During his long political career, he served as a congressman, secretary of war, vice president, senator, and secretary of state.

Chubby Checker (1941–) is best known as an early rock and roll star who created a song and a dance called "The Twist." He is from Spring Gulley.

Mary Boykin Chesnut (1823–1886) wrote a diary detailing her experiences during the Civil War. The diary also vividly describes Southern society, making it a valuable source for learning about life in the South at the time. Chesnut lived on a plantation in Camden.

Septima Poinsette Clark See page 70.

John C. Calhoun

Stephen Colbert (1964–), a native of Charleston, is an actor and comedian who first made a name for himself on the comedy show *The Daily Show*. In 2005, he began starring in his own show called *The Colbert Report*, in which he pokes fun at the self-important (including himself).

Pat Conroy See page 81.

Beth Daniel (1956–), who was born in Charleston, is a professional golfer. She was the 1979 Ladies Professional Golf Association (LPGA) Rookie of the Year and has since won more than 30 LPGA tournaments.

James Dickey (1923–1997) was a poet, novelist, and literary critic who lived in South Carolina most of his adult life. His novels include *Buckdancer's Choice*, which earned a National Book Award.

Larry Doby (1923–2003) became the second African American to play in Major League Baseball when he joined the Cleveland Indians in 1947. He was elected to the National Baseball Hall of Fame in 1998. He was born in Camden.

Stephen Colbert

Beth Daniel

Marian Wright Edelman See page 94.

James D. Elliott Jr. See page 21.

Robert B. Elliott See page 59.

Alex English (1954–) was one of the National Basketball Association's leading scorers during the 1980s. Born in Columbia, he played for the Denver Nuggets.

Joe Frazier See page 82.

Kevin Garnett (1976–) is a National Basketball Association all-star. A 6-foot-11 (211 cm) power forward, he spent most of his career with the Minnesota Timberwolves before moving to the Boston Celtics, where he led the team to a national championship in 2008 against the rival Los Angeles Lakers. He is from Mauldin.

Leeza Gibbons (1957–) of Hartsville has hosted TV shows such as *Entertainment Tonight*, *Extra*, and *Leeza*.

Althea Gibson See page 83.

Dizzy Gillespie See page 80.

Sarah Grimke and **Angelina Grimke Weld** See page 52.

DuBose Heyward (1885–1940) wrote the book *Porgy*, which was adapted into the folk opera *Porgy and Bess* by George Gershwin. He was from Charleston.

Ernest "Fritz" Hollings (1922–) served as governor of South Carolina from 1959 to 1963 and as a U.S. senator from 1966 to 2005. He was born in Charleston.

Charlayne Hunter-Gault (1942–) is a reporter who has worked for PBS, the *New York Times*, the *New Yorker*, and National Public Radio. She was born in Due West.

Andrew Jackson See page 93.

Jesse Jackson (1941–) is a civil rights leader who ran for president in 1984 and 1988. He was born in Greenville.

"Shoeless Joe" Jackson See page 114.

Eartha Kitt (1927–) is a singer and actor of African American and Cherokee heritage. Her hits include "Santa Baby" from 1953. During the 1960s, she played the role of Catwoman in the *Batman* TV series. She was born in North, a town in central South Carolina.

Francis Marion See page 49.

Eartha Kitt

Mary-Louise Parker

Ronald E. McNair (1950–1986), who was born in Lake City, was a physicist and astronaut. He was killed when the space shuttle *Challenger* exploded shortly after takeoff.

Roger Milliken See page 102.

Robert Mills (1781–1855) was an architect who designed the Washington Monument, the U.S. Department of Treasury building, and other notable structures throughout the nation. He was born in Charleston.

Margaret "Peggy" Parish (1927–1988) is the creator of the Amelia Bedelia series of children's books. She was raised in Manning and attended the University of South Carolina.

Mary-Louise Parker (1964–) is an actor who has appeared in movies such as *Mr. Wonderful*, *The Client*, and *The Spiderwick Chronicles*. She is from Fort Jackson.

William Perry (1962–) played football with the Chicago Bears for eight years and the Philadelphia Eagles for one year. A native of Aiken, he was nicknamed the Refrigerator because of his size.

Charles C. Pinckney (1746–1825) was a diplomat who helped write the U.S. Constitution. He was from Charleston.

Eliza Lucas Pinckney (1722–1793) was an entrepreneur who introduced the indigo plant to South Carolina. Born in the West Indies, she moved to the Charleston area as a child.

Darius Rucker (1966–) is a musician who served as lead singer for the band Hootie and the Blowfish and then began a solo country career in 2008. He is from Charleston.

John Rutledge (1739–1800) was the second chief justice of the U.S. Supreme Court. He also signed the U.S. Constitution and served as governor of South Carolina. He was from Charleston.

Robert Smalls See page 55.

Thomas Sumter (1734–1832) was born in Virginia and moved to South Carolina as an adult. He was a businessman and plantation owner. During the American Revolution, he served as a lieutenant colonel and gained the nickname the Gamecock for his feisty fighting style.

Darius Rucker

Strom Thurmond (1902–2003), from Edgefield, served as governor from 1947 to 1951. In 1954, he became the first and only U.S. senator to win election as a write-in candidate. When he retired from the Senate in 2003, at age 100, he had become the oldest senator in U.S. history.

Jean Hoefer Toal See page 92.

Charles Hard Townes (1915–) won the 1964 Nobel Prize in Physics for his work in quantum physics, particularly laser devices. He is from Greenfield.

William Westmoreland (1914–2005) served as the commander of U.S. military forces in South Vietnam for four years during the Vietnam War. He was from Spartanburg and was educated at the Citadel.

Vanna White (1957–) is a TV personality best known for her role on the game show *Wheel of Fortune*. She was born in North Myrtle Beach.

Jonathan J. Wright See page 58.

Vanna White

RESERVES

BOOKS

Nonfiction

Cooper, Michael L. *From Slave to Civil War Hero: The Life and Times of Robert Smalls*. New York: Dutton Juvenile, 1994.

Hasan, Heather. *A Primary Source History of the Colony of South Carolina*. New York: Rosen Central, 2005.

Jerome, Kate Boehm. *Civil War Sub: The Mystery of the Hunley*. New York: Grosset & Dunlap, 2002.

Kaufman, Scott. *Francis Marion: Swamp Fox of South Carolina*. Stockton, N.J.: OTTN Publishing, 2006.

Sherrow, Victoria. *Uniquely South Carolina*. Chicago: Heinemann, 2004.

Worth, Richard. *South Carolina: Life in the Thirteen Colonies*. Danbury, Conn.: Children's Press, 2004.

Fiction

Kidd, Sue Monk. *The Secret Life of Bees*. New York: Penguin Books, 2003.

Lavender, William. *Just Jane: A Daughter of England Caught in the Struggle of the American Revolution*. New York: Gulliver Books, 2002.

Love, D. Anne. *Three Against the Tide*. New York: Yearling, 2000.

Reeder, Carolyn. *Before the Creeks Ran Red*. New York: HarperCollins, 2003.

Weston, Elise. *The Coastwatcher*. Atlanta: Peachtree Publishing, 2005.

Woodson, Jacqueline. *Show Way*. New York: Putnam Books, 2005.

DVDs

American Experience: The Massachusetts 54th Colored Infantry. WGBH Boston, 2006.
Discoveries … America: South Carolina. Bennett-Watt Entertainment, Inc., 2004.
Elfego Baca and The Swamp Fox: Legendary Heroes. Walt Disney Treasures, 2005.
Hunt for the USS Alligator. Discovery Channel, 2007.

WEB SITES AND ORGANIZATIONS

South Carolina—The American Revolution
www.sciway.net/hist/periods/revolwar.html
Learn about key battles in South Carolina,
along with military officers and soldiers.

South Carolina Government
www.sc.gov
For information from the state of South
Carolina.

South Carolina Information Highway
www.sciway.net/
This is the largest directory of South Carolina
information on the Internet.

South Carolina Legislature
www.scstatehouse.net
To find information about the South Carolina
General Assembly.

South Carolina Tourism
http://discoversouthcarolina.com
Read all about what there is to do in South
Carolina.

INDEX

★ ★ ★

AUTHOR'S TIPS AND SOURCE NOTES

★　★　★

Research for this book began at the Greenville Library System's South Carolina Reading Room. The room contains a collection of historic documents, diaries, and journals from throughout the state. Greenville is one of South Carolina's largest cities, and the library has an extensive collection of histories, travel guides, and literature. Interesting South Carolina diaries used in this book include *The Nineteenth Century Diary of Greenville, South Carolina* by Laura Smith Ebaugh; *The 1860 Diary of Lemuel Reid*; and *The Diary of Keziah Goodwyn Hopkins Brevard, 1860-1861*.

I also read *Colonial South Carolina: A History* by Robert M. Weir; *South Carolina: A History* by Walter Edgar; *History of South Carolina* by Robert Lathan and S. Robert Lathan; and *The South Carolina Encyclopedia* edited by Walter Edgar. These books provide a comprehensive picture of the state.

Web sites that were particularly helpful in researching South Carolina include the South Carolina government site (www.sc.gov), the South Carolina Department of Natural Resources (www.dnr.sc.gov), and the tourism site (www.discoversouthcarolina.com). A good source for the colonial days is the Revolutionary War site (www.sciway.net/hist/periods/revolwar.html), which is part of the South Carolina Information Highway (www.sciway.net). Try www.awod.com/cwchas/firstper.html for primary source information about the Civil War, as well as the Duke University Civil War Women site (http://library.duke.edu/specialcollections/bingham/guides/cwdocs.html).

Photographs © 2009: age fotostock/Robert W. Ginn: 17; Alamy Images: 14 (Pat & Chuck Blackley), 109 top (Pat Canova), 21 bottom (Eric Horan), 113, 114 right (Andre Jenny), 85 center (JupiterImages/Brand X), 89 (Dennis MacDonald), 33 top right, 38, 42, 52, 55 (North Wind Picture Archives), 4 top left, 9 right, 18, 120 (David Osborn), 112 top (Bob Pardue); AP Images: 94 bottom (Vandell Cobb/Ebony Collection), 134 bottom (Jonathan Hayward), 130 center (Paula Illingworth), 92 left (Lou Krasky), 73 right, 76 (Diedra Laird/The Charlotte Observer), 133 top (NASA), 94 top (Ken Ruinard/Anderson Independent-Mail); Art Resource, NY: 4 top center, 23 bottom, 25, 122 top (Werner Forman), 78 (Jacques Lemoyne, c. de Morgues/The Pierpont Morgan Library), 4 top right, 33 bottom (Snark), 26, 30 top (John White/British Museum); Bridgeman Art Library International Ltd., London/New York: 23 top right, 28 (British Museum, London, UK/Boltin Picture Library), 49 bottom (Chicago History Museum, USA), 51 (Private Collection/Peter Newark American Pictures); Courtesy of the Charleston Raptor Center: 21 top; Corbis Images: back cover, 45 top right, 59 top, 68, 82 top (Bettmann), 5 bottom, 110 top (Richard Bickel), 72, 73 left (Broudy/Donohue Photography), 86, 87 left (Tami Chappell/Reuters), 98, 99 left (Ed Eckstein), 4 bottom left, 85 bottom (Envision), 60 top, 61 top left (E.O. Hoppe), 134 top (Lucas Jackson/Reuters), 5 top right, 70 (Karen Kasmauski), 133 bottom (Charles Bird King/The Corcoran Gallery of Art), 99 right, 103 (Bob Krist), 135 bottom (Andrew Marks), 81 (Matthew Mendelsohn), 80 bottom, 80 top (Michael Ochs Archives), 66 (Gordon Parks), 109 bottom (Tony Roberts), 136 bottom (Mark Savage), 19 (Michael T. Sedam), 121 (Thinkstock), cover inset (George Tiedemann/GT Images), 108 (Steven Vidler/Eurasia Press), 41 (Nik Wheeler), 5 top left, 53, 54, 58 bottom, 65; Digital Railroad/Tom Bean: 111; Getty Images: 63 (Archive Holdings Inc.), 135 top (Djamilla Rosa Cochran), 93 right (FPG), 82 bottom (Grant Halverson), 61 top right, 71 (Chris Hondros), 13 (Eric Horan), 32 top, 33 top left (Hulton Archive), 67 (Jorgen Juncker Jensen), 83 (Keystone), 102 (Rob Kinmonth), 92 right, 93 left (Stephen Morton), 59 bottom (MPI), 114 left (National Baseball Hall of Fame Library), 60 bottom, 124 top (Inga Spence/Visuals Unlimited), 85 top (Tetra Images); Inmagine: 4 bottom right, 87 right, 96, 127; iStockphoto: 116 bottom, 130 bottom (Geoffrey Black), 130 top (David Freund), 5 center, 44 bottom, 123 (Hannamaria Photography), 128 (Vladislav Lebedinski); JupiterImages: 61 bottom, 124 bottom; Library of Congress: 62; Lonely Planet Images: 110 bottom (Stephen Saks), 100 (Oliver Strewe); NEWSCOM/Bill Greenblatt/UPI: 136 top; North Wind Picture Archives: 34, 36, 44 top, 45 top left; Superstock, Inc.: 115 (Bill Barley), cover main (Dean Fox), 8, 9 left (Ferrell McCollough), 22 bottom (Museum of Natural Antiquities); The Art Archive/Picture Desk: 39; The Granger Collection, New York: 22 top, 23 top left, 30 bottom, 32 bottom, 40, 43, 45 bottom, 47, 49 top, 57, 58 top, 122 bottom; Tom Dietrich: 12; Transparencies Inc.: 84, 112 bottom (Jane Faircloth), 79, 132 (Michael Moore); US Mint: 116 top, 119; Vector-Images.com: 97, 126.

Maps by Map Hero, Inc.